D0881835

THE GREEK HISTORIANS

LITERATURE AND HISTORY

Ἐσθλὸν τοῖσι σοφοῖσι σοφίζεσθαι κατὰ τέχνεν

Dedications from the Athenian
Akropolis, no. 224.

THE GREEK HISTORIANS

LITERATURE AND HISTORY

PAPERS PRESENTED TO
A.E. RAUBITSCHEK

ANMA LIBRI

DEPARTMENT OF CLASSICS, STANFORD UNIVERSITY

Preface

Toni Raubitschek's seventieth birthday might well have been celebrated with a conference on the archaeology or epigraphy of Athens
or on ancient political philosophy—or on the conjunction of poetry,
art and religion seen in the dedications of the Greeks, as Joseph Day's
paper reminds us. But the appropriateness of the Greek historians
as our subject needs no defense when one notes that six of the con-
tributors to this volume have been Toni's pupils. At Yale, at Princeton
and here at Stanford, where he teamed up with Lionel Pearson, his
strongest scholarly influence has been on the reading of the Greek
historians—or so it seems to one who wishes he had had the privilege
of studying under him. Perhaps this has come about because in the
Greek historians are combined intellect, art and a stubborn sense of
historical reality, in a balance which it is as difficult for the critic to
preserve as for the historian to achieve. To understand the historians
and pass this understanding on has been a challenge to which Toni
has always responded with joy.

The first years after the Second World War were marked by the
rewarding application of the new knowledge produced by archaeology
and epigraphy to the study of Greek history. Fifth-century Athens
was the focus, and one thinks of the many publications of Benjamin
Meritt and of all those who at various times have been his associates,
including of course Toni Raubitschek. The scholarship of more recent years has begun to return to the appreciation of the Greek

historians themselves as inquirers, selectors, interpreters and above all writers. Classical scholarship has revived old problems and methods but has also shared in the current interest in the nature of texts and the theory of their study. At the same time in historical studies interest in ancient society and economy has led to a greater awareness of those groups whose voices are not heard among the cultivated accents of our literary texts but whose presence determined the character of Greek history and Greek society — barbarians (notably the Persians), women, slaves. These impulses have stimulated a spate of publications which make the study of the Greek historians one of the most productive areas in Classical studies.

Among the less obvious benefits of working at Stanford is the torrent of internal communications we receive via the departmental mailboxes, especially if one's box adjoins Toni Raubitschek's. It was a couple of years ago that Toni responded to my loan of one of these elegant and ingenious new treatises with a page of lively comments from which I quote the essential sentence: "The gentle reader, and perhaps even the author, forgets that he is dealing with *genomena* — historical events — and is persuaded, or persuades himself, that all there is are *legomena* or *nooumena* — things said and thought." In the light of Toni's warning, one may wonder if the pendulum has swung too far in this direction. It was the delicate and intricate relationship of things said and thought to things done that provided the theme for this conference.

In the event, the discussion of the papers, formally and informally in the course of two rare sunny days in a season of flood, proved to be as vigorous and as diverse as the views of the speakers themselves, thanks in part to the invited commentators — Paul Robinson (whose developed discussion of W.R. Connor's paper is included here), R.S. Stroud, J.K. Anderson, Raphael Sealey and Lionel Pearson. It is to share the papers with a wider audience that the Department of Classics has undertaken their publication. Of the papers delivered, however, Sir Ronald Syme has preferred to keep his oral.

For the holding of the conference, attended by over a hundred from near and far, and for preparing this publication our debts are many — first to the speakers who responded promptly and generously to our invitation; to Jack Winkler who saw to the smooth functioning of the conference itself; to Dirk Obbink who, with the assistance of Isabelle Raubitschek and Joshua Sommer, compiled the Bibliography; to Laurie Obbink, Dirk Obbink, Virginia Jameson and Mary Lou Munn for editing the papers; to Kay Hanner and Ann Arevalo in the Classics Department office for preparing the manuscripts for publication; and to Andrew Devine for turning the manuscripts into a book. Anastasia Oung made a notable gift in memory of her father, M.C. Oung, for which we are most grateful. We also owe thanks for support to Ian Watt, Director of the Stanford Humanities Center, to Norman Wessells, Dean of Humanities and Sciences at Stanford, and to Marsh McCall, chairman of the department, for his many good offices and for making available the resources of the Classics Department gift fund.

Michael H. Jameson
Stanford, December 1983

Contents

Bibliography of
Antony E. Raubitschek

1935

Epikureische Untersuchungen, unpublished dissertation (Wien 1935).

1936

'Bericht über Zusammensetzungen archaischer Inschriftensteine von der Akropolis in Athen', *Anzeiger der Akademie der Wissenschaften in Wien* 73 (1936), 29-30.

1937

5 articles in *Paulys Realencyclopädie der classischen Altertumswissenschaft*, vol. 17.2 (1937): Oiagros, Oianthe, Oinobios, Oinophilos, Oionokles.

1938

16 articles in *Paulys Realencyclopädie der classischen Altertumswissenschaft*, vol. 19.2 (1938): Phainarete, Phainippos, Phanagores, Phanas, Phanion, Phano, Phanomachos, Phanope, Phanosthenes, Phanostrate, Phanostratos, Pharnapates, Pharnaspes, Phayllos, Pheidippos, Philoktemon.

'Zur Technik und Form der altattischen Statuenbasen', *Bulletin de l'Institut Archéologique Bulgare* 12 (1938), 132-181.

'Zu einigen Wiederholungen bei Lukrez', *American Journal of Philology* 59:2 (1938), 218-223.

'Zu altattischen Weihinschriften', *Jahreshefte des Oesterreichischen Archäologischen Instituts in Wien* 31 (1938), 21-68.

1939

Article in *Paulys Realencyclopädie der classischen Altertumswissenschaft*, vol. 18 (1939): Onetor.

'*Erga megala te kai thomasta*', *Revue des Études Anciennes* 41:3 (1939), 217-222.

'Leagros', *Hesperia* 8:2 (1939), 155-164.

'Early Attic Votive Monuments', *Annual of the British School at Athens* 40 (1939), 17-37.

Review of E. Loewy, *Zur Datierung attischer Inschriften*, and *Der Beginn der rotfigurigen Vasenmalerei*, in *American Journal of Archaeology* 43:4 (1939), 710-713.

1940

'The Inscription on the Base of the Athena Promachos Statue', *American Journal of Archaeology* 44:1 (1940), 109.

'Two Monuments erected after the Victory of Marathon', *American Journal of Archaeology* 44:1 (1940), 53-59.

'Some Notes on Early Attic Stoichedon Inscriptions', *Journal of Hellenic Studies* 60 (1940), 50-59.

'A New Fragment of A.T.L., D8', *American Journal of Philology* 61:4 (1940), 475-479.

1941

9 articles in *Paulys Realencyclopädie der classischen Altertumswissenschaft*, vol. 20.1 (1941): Philon, Philonides, Philytas, Phokides, Phryne, Phrygia, Phrynichos, Phrynis, Phrynoi.

'Note on a Study of the Acropolis Dedications', *American Journal of Archaeology* 45:1 (1941), 70.

'The Heroes of Phyle', *Hesperia* 10:3 (1941), 284-295.

'A Possible Signature of Kalamis', *American Journal of Archaeology* 45:1 (1941), 90.

'Two Notes on Isocrates', *Transactions of the American Philological Association* 72 (1941), 356-364.

1942

Two articles in *Paulys Realencyclopädie der classischen Altertumswissenschaft*, vol. 18.2 (1942): Orthobulos, Oulios.

'Notes on Attic Prosopography', *Hesperia* 11:3 (1942), 304-313.

'The Potter Relief from the Akropolis', *American Journal of Archaeology* 46:1 (1942), 123.

'An Original Work of Endoios', *American Journal of Archaeology* 46:2 (1942), 245-253.

'*I.G.* II², 2839 and 2844', *Classical Philology* 37:3 (1942), 317-319.

Review of W.K. Pritchett and B.D. Meritt, *The Chronology of Hellenistic Athens*, in *American Journal of Archaeology* 46:4 (1942), 574-575.

1943

'Greek Inscriptions', *Hesperia* 12:1 (1943), 12-96.

'The Inscriptions', in *Small Objects from the Pnyx*: I, ed. G.R. Davidson and D.B. Thompson, *Hesperia: Supplement* 7 (1943), 1-11.

'Heinrich Gomperz', *American Journal of Archaeology* 47:2 (1943), 227-228.

1944

'A Note on *I.G.* I², 945', *Hesperia* 13:4 (1944), 352.

'Athens and Halikyai', *Transactions of the American Philological Association* 75 (1944), 10-14.

Review of L. Pearson, *The Local Historians of Attica*, in *American Journal of Philology* 45:3 (1944), 294-297.

Review of W.A. McDonald, *The Political Meeting Places of the Greeks*, in *American Historical Review* 49:3 (1944), 692-694.

Review of C.E. Black, *The Establishment of Constitutional Government in Bulgaria*, in *Russian Review* 4:1 (1944), 118-120.

1945

'A Greek Folksong copied for Lord Byron', *Hesperia* 14:1 (1945), 33-35 (with C.M. Dawson).

'*Kynebion-Kys*', *Record of the Museum of Historic Art*, Princeton University 4:1 (1945), 9-10.

'Hadrian as Son of Zeus Eleutherios', *American Journal of Archaeology* 49:2 (1945), 128-133.

'Two Notes on Athenian Epigrams', *Hesperia* 14:4 (1945), 367-368.

'The Pyloroi of the Akropolis', *Transactions of the American Philological Association* 76 (1945), 104-107.

'The Priestess of Pandrosos', *American Journal of Archaeology* 49:4 (1945), 434-435.

Review of S.D. Markman, *The Horse in Greek Art*, in *American Journal of Philology* 46:2 (1945), 220-222.

Review of B. Newman, *Balkan Background*, in *The Philhellene* 4:4-5 (1945), 4.

Review of A.W. Parsons, *Klepsydra and the Paved Court of the Pythion*, in *American Journal of Archaeology* 49:2 (1945), 187-189.

Review of *Transactions and Proceedings of the American Philological Association* 74, (1943), in *American Journal of Philology* 46:3 (1945), 330-333.

1946

Hesperia: Index, Volumes I-X, Supplements I-IV: Epigraphical Indexes (American School of Classical Studies at Athens 1946).

'The Pedestal of the Athena Promachos', *Hesperia* 15:2 (1946), 107-114.

'Octavia's Deification in Athens', *Transactions of the American Philological Association* 77 (1946), 146-150.

Review of H. Bloesch, *Agalma, Kleinod, Weihgeschenk, Götterbild: Ein Beitrag zur frühgriechischen Kultur- und Religionsgeschichte*, in *American Journal of Ar-chaeology* 50:1 (1946), 196-197.

Review of E. Langlotz, *Die Darstellung des Menschen in der griechischen Kunst*, in *American Journal of Archaeology* 50:1 (1946), 197-198.

Review of E. Langlotz, *Über das Interpretieren griechischer Plastik*, in *American Journal of Archaeology* 50:1 (1946), 198.

Review of E. Langlotz, *Griechische Klassik*, in *American Journal of Archaeology* 50:1 (1946), 199.

1947

'The Ostracism of Xanthippos', in *American Journal of Archaeology* 51:3 (1947), 257-262.

'Three Attic Proxeny Decrees', *Hesperia* 16:2 (1947), 78-81 (with C.P. Loughran).

'Early Christian Epitaphs from Athens', *Hesperia* 16:1 (1947), 1-54 (with J.S. Creaghan).

'Jean Hatzfeld', *American Journal of Archaeology* 51:3 (1947), 305.

Early Christian Epitaphs from Athens, Woodstock, Maryland, 1947 (with J.S. Creaghan).

1948

'The Case against Alcibiades (Andocides IV)', *Transactions of the American Philological Association* 79 (1948), 191-210.

'Sophocles of Sunion', *Jahresheft des Oesterreichischen Archäologischen Instituts in Wein* 37 (1948), 35-40.

'Ostracism', *Archaeology* 1:1 (1948), 79-82.

Selected Works of Cicero, New York, 1948 (with I.K. Raubitschek and L.R. Loomis).

Review of A.P. Dorjahn, *Political Forgiveness in Old Athens: The Amnesty of 403 B.C.*, in *American Journal of Philology* 69:1 (1948), 126-127.

Review of E. Buschor, *Vom Sinn der griechischen Standbilder*, in *American Journal of Archaeology* 52:2 (1948), 414-415.

1949

Supplementum Epigraphicum Graecum, vol. 10, (Lugduni Batavorum 1949), edd. A.E. Raubitschek and J.J.E. Hondius.

'Commodus and Athens', in *Commemorative Studies in Honor of Theodore Leslie Shear*, *Hesperia: Supplement* 8 (1949), 279-290.

'Phaidros and his Roman Pupils', *Hesperia* 18:1 (1949), 96-103.

Dedications from the Athenian Akropolis, Cambridge, Mass., 1949 (with L.H. Jeffery); pp. 433-453 reprinted in German translation as 'Einige technische Bemerkungen zu den frühen attischen Weihungen', in *Das Alphabet*, 'Wege der Forschung' 88 (Darmstadt 1968), 339-434.

Review of H.A. Bauer, *Das antike Athen in zwanzig Farbaufnahmen*, in *American Journal of Archaeology* 53:1-2 (1949), 84 and 219-220.

Review of H. Bogner, *Der tragische Gegensatz*, in *Classical Philology* 44:2 (1949), 131-132.

Review of F.R. Cowell, *Cicero and the Roman Republic*, in *American Historical Review* 55:1 (1949), 105-106.

1950

Excavations at Gözlü Kule, Tarsus, I: The Hellenistic and Roman Periods, The Inscriptions (Princeton 1950), 384-387.

'Toynbee and the Classics', *Classical Weekly* 43:7 (1950), 99-100.

'Another Drachma Dedication', *Yale Classical Studies* 11 (1950), 295-296.

'The Crisis of the Athenian Democracy', *Transactions of the American Philological Association* 80 (1950), 434-435.

'The Origin of Ostracism', *American Journal of Archaeology* 55:3 (1950), 258-259.

Review of A. Lesky, *Thalatta: Der Weg der Griechen zum Meer*, in *American Journal of Archaeology* 55:1 (1950), 92-93.

Review of J.A. Notopoulos, *The Platonism of Shelley*, in *Thought* 25 (1950), 253-255.

Review of G.M.A. Richter, *Archaic Greek Sculpture*, in *Saturday Review of Literature* 23:1 (1950), 37-38.

Review of W.H.D. Rouse, *Homer, The Iliad and the Odyssey*, in *Princeton Alumni Weekly* 50 (1950), no. 28 (*Good Reading* 1:2).

1951

'The Mechanical Engraving of Circular Letters', *American Journal of Archaeology* 55:3 (1951), 343-344; reprinted in *Festschrift A. Rumpf zum 60. Geburtstag* (Krefeld 1951), 125-126.

'Sylleia', in *Studies in Honor of A.C. Johnson* (Princeton 1951), 49-57.

'The Origin of Ostracism', *American Journal of Archaeology* 55:2 (1951), 221-229.

'The Key to the Classical Tradition', *Vanderbilt Alumnus* 37:2 (1951), 12-16.

Review of C. Bonner, *Studies in Magical Amulets*, in *American Journal of Archaeology* 55:4 (1951), 419-420.

Review of F. Jacoby, *Atthis: The Local Chronicles of Ancient Athens*, in *Classical Weekly* 44:9 (1951), 135.

Review of J.H. Oliver, *The Athenian Expounders of the Sacred and Ancestral Law*, in *Classical Weekly* 44:9 (1951), 135-136.

Review of G.M.A. Richter, *Archaic Greek Sculpture*, in *Princeton Alumni Weekly* 52 (1951), no. 8 (*Good Reading* 3:1).

Review of K. Schefold, *Orient, Hellas, und Rom in die archäologischen Forschung seit 1939*, in *Classical Philology* 46:1 (1951), 62-63.

Review of W. Schmalenbach, *Griechische Vasenbilder*, and K. Schefold, *Griechische Plastik, I: Die grossen Bildhauer des archaiischen Athen*, in *American Journal of Philology* 72:2 (1951), 213-14.

Review of F. Solmsen, *Hesiod and Aeschylus*, in *Classical Weekly* 45:5 (1951), 70-72.

1952

'Plato's College', *Classical Weekly* 45:13 (1952), 193-196.

'International Epigraphy: Report on the Second International Congress of Greek and Latin Epigraphy, Paris, April 15-19, 1952, *Archaeology* 5:2 (1952), 119-120.

'When History was Young', *Classical Bulletin* 28:5 (1952), 49-52, 62-65, 68.

Review of A. Calderini, *L'Ostracismo*, in *Classical Philology* 47:3 (1952), 203-204.

Review of D. Grene, *Man in His Pride: A Study in the Political Philosophy of Thucydides and Plato*, in *Classical Weekly* 46:3 (1952), 40.

Review of B.D. Meritt, H.T. Wade-Gery, and M.F. McGregor, *The Athenian Tribute Lists*, in *Classical Weekly* 45:15 (1952), 230-231.

Review of W.T. Stace, *Religion and the Modern Mind*, in *Daily Princetonian* 76 (1952), no. 138.

1953

'Notes on the Post-Hadrianic Boule', in *Geras Antoniou Keramopoullou* (Athens 1953), 242-255.

'Two Notes on the Fasti of Achaia', in *Studies presented to D.M. Robinson, II* (St. Louis 1953), 330-333.

'Ostracism: The Athenian Ostraca', in *Actes du 2e Congrès International d'Épigraphie Grecque* (Paris 1953), 59-74.

'Education and the Classics: Unaided Reason', *Folia* 7:2 (1953), 86-107.

'Athenian Ostracism', *Classical Journal* 48:4 (1953), 113-122.

Review of H.R. Breitenbach, *Historiographische Anschauungsformen Xenophons*, in *Classical Philology* 48:1 (1953), 36-37.

Review of E. Buschor, *Frühgriechische Jünglinge*, in *Archaeology* 6:3 (1953), 187-188.

Review of M. Grant, *Roman Anniversary Issues: An Exploratory Study of the Numismatic and Medallic Commemoration of Anniversary Years, 49 B.C. - A.D. 375*, in *Classical Journal* 48:6 (1953), 271-272.

Review of R. Hampe, *Die Gleichnisse Homers und die Bildkunst seiner Zeit*, in *Archaeology* 6:1 (1953), 62.

Review of *Studies Presented to D.M. Robinson*, ed. G.E. Mylonas, in *Archaeology* 6:4 (1953), 254.

Review of C.J. Radcliffe, *The Problem of Power*, in *Princeton Alumni Weekly* 53 (1953), no. 26 (*Good Reading* 4:3).

1954

'The New Homer', *Hesperia* 23:4 (1954), 317-319.

'Philinos', *Hesperia* 23:4 (1954), 68-71.

'Epigraphical Notes on Julius Caesar', *Journal of Roman Studies* 44 (1954), 65-75.

'The Dates of Caesar's Second and Third Dictatorship', *American Journal of Archaeology* 58.2 (1954), 148.

'Der Ostrakismos des Theseus', *Bulletin d'archéologie et d'histoire Dalmate* 56-59:2 (1954), 50-51 (Mélanges Abramiĉ II).

'The Classics and the Bible', *Classical Bulletin* 30:4 (1954), 37-39.

'Values and Value Judgement', *Princeton Alumni Weekly* 54 (1954), no. 18.

Euripides' *Trojan Women* (translation), in *Anthology of Greek Drama* (New York 1954), 199-239.

Review of J.A. Oliver, *The Ruling Power: A Study of the Roman Empire in the Second Century after Christ through the Roman Oration of Aelius Aristides*, in *Phoenix* 8:4 (1954), 165-166.

Review of M. Rambaud, *L'Art de la déformation historique dans les Commentaires de César*, in *Latomus* 13 (1954), 615-616.

Review of A. Rumpf, *Archäologie*, in *Archaeology* 7:3 (1954), 187.

Review of A. Schmitt, *Der Buchstabe H im Griechischen*, in *Gnomon* 26:2 (1954), 121-122.

Review of W. Steidle, *Sueton und die antike Biographie*, in *Classical Philology* 49:1 (1954), 62-63.

Review of A.E. Taylor, *Socrates*, in *Princeton Alumni Weekly* 54 (1954), no. 18 (*Good Reading* 5:2).

1955

'Zur attischen Genealogie', *Rheinisches Museum* 98:3 (1955), 258-262.

'Damon', *Classica et Mediaevalia* 16:1-2 (1955), 78-83.

'Philochoros *Frag.* 36 (Jacoby)', *Hermes* 83:1 (1955), 119-120.

'Theopompos on Hyperbolos', *Phoenix* 9:3 (1955), 122-126.

'Gyges in Herodotus', *Classical Weekly* 48:4 (1955), 48-50.

'Menon, Son of Menekleides', *Hesperia* 24:4 (1955), 286-289.

'Aeschylus: *The Oresteia*', *Alumnae Bulletin*, Randolf-Macon Woman's College 49:1 (1955), 21-33.

Review of N. DeWitt, *St. Paul and Epicurus*, in *Princeton Alumni Weekly* 56 (1955), no. 8 (*Good Reading* 7:1).

Review of H.A. Musurillo, ed., *The Acts of the Pagan Martyrs, Acta Alexandrinorum*, in *Thought* 30 (1955), 446-447.

Review of *Heinrich Gomperz, Philosophical Studies*, ed. D.S. Robinson, in *Classical Weekly* 48:13 (1955), 184.

1956

'The Gates in the Agora', *American Journal of Archaeology* 60:3 (1956), 279-282.

'(H)abronichos', *Classical Review* 6:3-4 (1956), 199-200.

Review of *Miss Mabel's Oresteia*, in *Alumnae Bulletin*, Randolf-Macon Woman's College 49:2 (1956), 14.

Review of A. Aymard and J. Auboyer, *L'Orient et la Grèce antique*, in *Erasmus* 9:9-10 (1956), coll. 302-303.

Review of J. Pieper, *Justice*, in *Princeton Alumni Weekly* 56 (1956), no. 3 (*Good Reading* 7:3).

1957

'Die Verstossung des Themistokles', *Hermes* 84:4 (1957), 500-501.

'Brutus in Athens', *Phoenix* 11:1 (1957), 1-11.

'Das Datislied', *Charites E. Langlotz: Studien zur Altertumswissenschaft* (Bonn 1957), 234-242.

'Die schamlose Ehefrau', *Rheinisches Museum* 100:2 (1957), 139-140.

Review of Z. Gansiniec, *Geneza tropaionu*, in *Archaeology* 10:4 (1957), 295-296.

Review of G. Klaffenbach, *Griechische Epigraphik*, in *Deutsche Literaturzeitung* 78:8 (1957), coll. 685-689.

Review of C.S. Lewis, *Till We Have Faces: A Myth Retold*, in *Princeton Alumni Weekly* 57 (1957), no. 26 (*Good Reading* 8:3).

Review of A. Rumpf, *Archäologie* II, in *Archaeology* 10:4 (1957), 292-293.

1958

'Meeresnähe und Volksherrschaft', *Wiener Studien* 71 (1958), 112-115.

'Theophrastos on Ostracism', *Classica et Mediaevalia* 19:1-2 (1958), 73-109.

'Ein neues Pittakeion', *Wiener Studien* 71 (1958), 170-172.

Review of *The Christian Idea of Education*, ed. E. Fuller, in *Princeton Alumni Weekly* 59 (1958), no. 9 (*Good Reading* 10:1).

Review of M.P. Nilsson, *Die hellenistische Schule*, in *Phoenix* 12:1 (1958), 40-42.

Review of *Ovid's Art of Love*, in *Princeton Alumni Weekly* 58 (1958), no. 26 (*Good Reading* 9:3).

1959

'The Brutus Statue in Athens', *Atti del III Congresso Internazionale di Epigrafia Greca e Latina* (Rome 1959), 15-21.

'Arae Augusti', *Hesperia* 28:1 (1959), 65-85 (with Anna Benjamin).

'A Note on the Inscription on the Plaster Cast', *Record of the Art Museum*, Princeton University 18:2 (1959), 60.

'Die Rükkehr des Aristeides', *Historia* 8 (1959), 127-128.

Review of F.E. Adcock, *Roman Political Ideas and Practice*, in *Classical World* 52:8 (1959), 256.

Review of *Monumenta Asiae Minoris Antiqua* VII, ed. W.M. Calder (II), in *Journal of Biblical Literature* 78:4 (1959), 359-361.

Review of R. Flacelière, *Inscriptions de la terrasse du temple et de la région nord du sanctuaire* (Fouilles de Delphes 3,4), and J. Marcadé, *Recueil des signatures de sculpteurs grecs*, I, in *Gnomon* 31:3 (1959), 266-268.

Review of *C. Julii Caesaris Commentarii De bello civili*, edd. F. Kraner and F. Hoffmann, in *Classical World* 53:2 (1959), 59 (with I.K. Raubitschek).

Review of N.A. Maschkin, *Zwischen Republik und Kaiserreich: Ursprung und sozialer Character des Augusteischen Prinzipats*, transl. M. Brandt, in *Erasmus* 12:11-12 (1959), coll. 361-362.

Review of E. Mireaux, *Daily Life in the Time of Homer*, transl. I. Sells, in *Classical World* 53:1 (1959), 13-14.

Review of H.W. Pleket, *The Greek Inscriptions in the "Rijksmuseum van Ouheden" at Leyden*, in *American Journal of Archaeology* 63:1 (1959), 99.

Review of F. Sartori, *La eterie nelle vita politica Ateniese del VI e V secolo A.C.*, in *American Journal of Philology* 80:1 (1959), 81-88.

1960

'Theopompos on Thucydides the Son of Melesias', *Phoenix* 14:2 (1960), 81-95.

'The Covenant of Platea', *Transactions of the American Philological Association* 91 (1960), 178-183.

Review of S.P. Bovie, *Horace's Satires and Epistles*, in *Yearbook of Comparative and General Literature* 9 (1960), 114-115.

1961

'Herodotus and the Inscriptions', *Bulletin of the Institute of Classical Studies*, University of London 8 (1961), 59-61.

Review of H.H. Scullard, *From the Gracchi to Nero: A History of Rome from 133 B.C. to A.D. 68*, in *Erasmus* 14:11-12 (1961), coll. 365-366.

Review of A. Severyns, *Grèce et Proche-Orient avant Homère*, in *Classical World* 55:1 (1961), 16.

1962

'Demokratia', *Hesperia* 31 (1962), 238-243.

Review of L.H. Jeffery, *The Local Scripts of Archaic Greece*, in *Gnomon* 34:3 (1962), 225-231; reprinted in *Das Alphabet*, 'Wege der Forschung' 88 (Darmstadt 1968), 435-444.

Review of H. Meyer, *Die Aussenpolitik des Augustus und die augusteische Dichtung*, in *Classical World* 56:3 (1962), 86.

Review of F. Ollier, *Xenophon, Banquet, Apologie de Socrate*, in *Classical World* 55:6 (1962), 170.

Review of J.N. Sevenster, *Paul and Seneca*, in *Classical World* 55:8 (1962), 260.

Review of C.G. Starr, *The Origins of Greek Civilization 1100-650 B.C.*, in *Gnomon* 34:2 (1962), 201-202.

1963

'War Melos tributpflichtig?', *Historia* 12:1 (1963), 78-83.

'The Marble Prohedria in the Theater of Dionysus', *American Journal of Archaeology* 67:2 (1963), 216.

'Ernst Buschor', *American Journal of Archaeology* 67:4 (1963), 421.

Review of U. Albini, *Andocide, L'orazione De Reditu*, in *American Journal of Philology* 84:3 (1963), 332-334.

Review of C.M. Eliot, *Coastal Demes of Attica: A Study in the Policy of Kleisthenes*, in *American Journal of Archaeology* 67:3 (1963), 313.

Review of A. Mannzmann, *Griechische Stiftungsurkunden: Studie zu Inhalt und Rechtsformen*, in *Classical Journal* 58:4 (1963), 185-186.

Review of A. Masaracchia, *Solone*, in *Classical Philology* 58:2 (1963), 137-140.

Review of B.D. Meritt, *The Athenian Year*, in *Phoenix* 17:2 (1963) 137-142.

1964

'Iamblichos at Athens', *Hesperia* 33:1 (1964), 63-68.

'Demokratia', in *Akte des IV. Internationalen Kongresses für Griechische und Lateinische Epigraphik* (Wien 1964), 332-337.

'Die Inschrift als Denkmal: Bermerkungen zur Methodologie der Inschriftkunde', *Studium Generale* 17:4 (1964), 219-228.

'The Treaties between Persia and Athens', *Greek, Roman, and Byzantine Studies* 5:3 (1964), 151-159.

Review of E. Badian, *Studies in Greek and Roman History*, in *Classical World* 58:2 (1964), 57.

Review of G. Gottlieb, *Das Verhältnis der ausserherodoteischen Überlieferung in Herodot*, in *Gnomon* 36:8 (1964), 829-830.

Review of R. Syme, *Sallust*, in *Classical World* 58:1 (1964), 21.

1965

'A Note on the Themistocles Decree', in *Studi in onore di Luisa Banti* (Rome 1965), 285-287.

'Die Inschrift als geschichtliches Denkmal', *Gymnasium* 72:6 (1965), 511-522.

'Hai Athenai tou Perikleous', *Epeteris tes philosophikes Scholes tou Panepistimou Athenon*, 1965, 101-124.

Review of B. Snell, *Scenes from Greek Drama*, in *Classical World* 58:8 (1965), 255-256.

1966

'The Peace Policy of Pericles', *American Journal of Archaeology* 70:1 (1966), 37-41.

'Otto Walter', *American Journal of Archaeology* 70:1 (1966), 74.

'Early Boeotian Potters', *Hesperia* 35:2 (1966), 154.

'Greek Inscriptions', *Hesperia* 35:3 (1966), 241-257.

'Zetemata Epigraphikes', *Epeteris tes philosophikes Scholes tou Panepistemiou Athenon*, 1966, 148-170.

Review of G.E. Bean and T.B. Mitford, *Journeys in Rough Cilicia in 1962 and 1963*, in *Anzeiger für die Altertumswissenschaft* 19:1 (1966), 70-71.

Review of L. Bieler, *The Grammarian's Craft: An Introduction to Textual Criticism*, in *Thought* 61 (1966), 455-458.

Review of R. Hutmacher, *Das Ehrendekret für den Strategen Kallimachos*, in *Gnomon* 38:8 (1966), 837-838.

Review of M.A. Levi, *Political Power in the Ancient World*, in *American Historical Review* 72:1 (1966), 137-138.

Review of H. Montgommery, *Gedanke und Tat: Zur Erzählungstechnik bei Herodot, Thucydides, Xenophon, und Arrian*, in *Classical World* 59:6 (1966), 197.

Review of L.D. Reynolds, ed., *L. Annaei Senecae ad Lucilium Epistulae Morales*, in *Classical World* 59:9 (1966), 321.

Review of F. Semi, *Il Semento di Cesare*, in *Classical World* 60:4 (1966), 166-167.

1967

Review of G. Pfohl, *Griechische Inschriften als Zeugnisse des privaten und öffentlichen Lebens*, in *Anzeiger für die Altertumswissenschaft* 20:4 (1967), 222-223.

1968

'Prokrisis', *Palingenesia* 4 (1968), 89-90.

Review of *The Classical Tradition: Literary and Historical Studies in Honor of Harry Caplan*, ed. L. Wallach, in *American Historical Review* 73:4 (1968), 1111-1112.

Review of R.M. Haywood, *Ancient Rome*, in *Classical World* 62:1 (1968), 24.

1969

'Das Denkmalepigramm', in *L'Epigramme Grecque, Entretiens sur l'antiquité classique*, Fondation Hardt XIV (Vandoevres-Genève 1968), 9-36.

'Drei Ostraka in Heidelberg', *Archäologischer Anzeiger* 1969, 107-108.

'Die attische Zwölfgötter', in *Opus Nobile: Festschrift zum 60. Geburtstag von U. Jantzen* (Wiesbaden 1969), 129-130.

Review of K. Buechner, *Sallustinterpretationen: In Auseinandersetzung mit dem Sallustbuch von Ronald Syme*, in *Classical World* 62:6 (1969), 228.

1970

'*IG* II 2314 + 13122 + *Hesperia Suppl.* VII Nr. 8', *Klio* 52 (1970), 379-381.

'The Cretan Inscription BM 1969, 4-2,1: A Supplementary Note', *Kadmos* 9:2 (1970), 155-156.

1971

'Inschriften als Hilfsmittel der Geschichtsforschung', *Rivista Storica dell' Antichità* 1:1-2 (1971), 177-195.

Review of F. Eckstein, *Anathemata: Studien zu den Weihgeschenken strengen Stils im Heiligtum von Olympia*, in *Erasmus* 23:6 (1971), 292-296.

1972

'A Late Byzantine Account of Ostracism', *American Journal of Philology* 93:1 (1972), 87-91 (with J.J. Keaney).

Early Cretan Armorers, Mainz, 1972 (with H. Hoffmann).

1973

'The Speech of the Athenians at Sparta', in *The Speeches in Thucydides*, ed. P.A. Stadter (Chapel Hill 1973), 32-48.

'Die sogenannten Interpolation in den ersten beiden Büchern von Xenophons griechischer Geschichte', *Vestigia* 17 (1973), 315-325.

'Kolieis', in *Phoros: Tribute to B.D. Meritt*, ed. D.W. Bradeen and M.F. McGregor (Locust Valley, New York 1974), 137-138.

'Der korinthische Sänger Pyrrhias', *Zeitschrift für Papyrologie und Epigraphik* 12:1 (1973), 99-100.

1974

'Eine Bermerkung zu Aristoteles, Verfassung von Athen 29, 2', *Chiron* 4 (1974), 101-102.

'Zu Periklesstatue des Kresilas', *Archeologia Classica* 25-26 (1974), 620-621 (*Volume in onore di M. Guarducci*).

'Zu den zwei attischen Marathondenkmälern in Delphi', in *Mélanges Helléniques offerts à Georges Daux* (Paris 1974), 315-316.

1975

'Nomos and Ethos', in *Classica et Iberica: A Festschrift in Honor of J.M.-F. Marique*.

'Der kretische Gürtel', in *Wandlungen: Studien zur antiken und neueren Kunst, E. Homann-Wedeking gewidmet* (Waldhassen-Bayern 1975), 49-52 (with Isabelle Raubitschek).

Review of E.F. Bloedow, *Alcibiades Reexamined*, in *Classical World* 68:6 (1975), 391.

1976

'Plato and Minos', *Quaderni di Storia* 3 (1976), 233-238.

'Epilogue', in *La Paz de Calias* by Carlos Schrader (Barcelona 1976), 215-217.

'*Me quoque excellentior (Boethii Consolatio* 4.6.27)', in *Latin Script and Letters A.D. 400-900: Festschrift Presented to L. Bieler* (Leiden 1976), 62.

1977

'Bermerkungen zu den Buchstabenformen der griechischen Inscriften des fünften Jahrhunderts', in *Das Studium der griechischen Epigraphik*, ed. G. Pfohl (Darmstadt 1977), 62-72.

'Bildhauerinschriften', in *Das Studium der griechischen Epigraphik*, ed. G. Pfohl (Darmstadt 1977), 116-120.

'Corinth and Athens before the Peloponnesian War', in *Greece and the Eastern Mediterranean in Ancient and Prehistory: Studies Presented to F. Schachermeyer* (Berlin 1977), 266-269.

Review of C. Mossé, *Athens in Decline 404-86 B.C.*, transl. J. Stewart, in *Classical World* 70:5 (1977), 341.

1979

'Attic Black-Figure Eye-Cup (Nikosthenic Workshop)', in *Greek Vase-Painting in Midwestern Collections* (Chicago 1979), 88-89.

1980

'Das Schwertband des Herakles', *Tainia: Roland Hampe zum 70. Geburtstag* (Mainz 1980), 65-67.

'Zum Ursprung und Wesen der Agonistik', in *Studien zur antiken Sozialgeschichte: Feschrift F. Vittinghoff* (Wien 1980), 1-5.

'Zu *Pap. Köln* 38 = Arch. *Fr.* 196A West', *Zeitschrift für Papyrologie und Epigraphik* 39 (1980), 48.

'Miscellanea: Theognis 313-314 and *Philoctetes* 1050-51', *Archaiognosia* 1:1 (1980), 188.

'Ein Peltast', *Grazer Beiträge* 9 (1980), 21-22.

1981

Inscriptiones Graecae: Inscriptiones Atticae Euclidis Anno Anteriores, vol. I, Editio Tertia, Fasc. I: Decreta et Tabulae Magistratum, Berlin, 1981 (ed. D. Lewis, with M.H. Jameson, A.E. Raubitschek, B.D. Meritt, M.F. McGregor, D.W. Bradeen, W.E. Thompson, A.G. Woodhead).

'Andocides and Thucydides', in *Classical Contributions: Studies in Honor of M.F. McGregor* (Locust Valley, New York 1981), 121-123.

'A New Attic Club (Eranos)', *J. Paul Getty Museum Journal* 9 (1981), 93-98.

1982

'The Dedication of Aristokrates', in *Studies in Attic Epigraphy, History and Topography Presented to Eugene Vanderpool, Hesperia: Supplement* 19 (1982), 130-132.

'The Mission of Triptolemos', in *Studies in Athenian Architecture, Sculpture and Topography Presented to Homer A. Thompson, Hesperia: Supplement* 20 (1982), 109-117 (with Isabelle Raubitschek).

'Die historische-politische Bedeutung der Parthenon und seiner Skulpturenschmuckes', *Parthenon-Kongress*, Basel 1982.

1983 foll.

'The Agonistic Spirit in Greek Culture', *Ancient World* 7:1-2 (1983), 3-7.

'Die Gründungsorakel der Dionysien', *Jahreshefte des Oesterreichischen Archäologischen Instituts, Festschrift für H. Kenner*.

'Philokaloumen met' Euteleias', 12th International Congress of Classical Archaeology, 1983.

'Theseus at the Isthmia', in *Festschrift D. Amyx*.

'Die Überschrift der ersten Tributquotaliste', in *Festschrift C.M. Danoff*.

'The Eleusinian Spondai (*I.G.* I³,6)', in *Festschrift G. Mylonas* (with Mariko Sakurai).

'Zur Frühgeschichte der Olympischen Spiele', in *Festschrift Hermann Vetters*.

Narrative Discourse in Thucydides

W. ROBERT CONNOR
Princeton University

The subject matter chosen for this gathering is appropriate not only to Toni Raubitschek's wide ranging interests, but also to a concern strongly felt in classical and historical studies and other humanistic fields as well. There are today many signs of a sea change in our understanding of the relationship between literature and history and hence in our understanding of the historians of the past and of historical writing in the present. Lawrence Stone drew attention to some of these signs a few years ago in an essay entitled "The Revival of Narrative."[1] Stone argued that there was a "noticeable shift of content, method and style among a very tiny, but disproportionately prominent, section of the historical profession."[2] The change was from what he called "structural" history to "narrative" history, that is to historical writing that is descriptive rather than analytical and whose central focus is on man and not on circumstances. He was not referring, of course, to the writing of antiquarians, or annalists, but to the shift from quantitative or "scientific" history toward another set of questions, especially those about the role of power and of the individual in history and also to the effort "to discover what was going on inside people's heads in the past, and what it was like to live in the past, questions which inevitably lead back to the use of narrative." Eric Hobsbawn in reply

---

[1] L. Stone, "The Revival of Narrative," *Past and Present* 85 (Nov. 1979) 3-23.
[2] Stone (above, note 1) 3.

challenged many of Stone's conclusions but conceded "there is evidence that the old historical avant-garde no longer rejects, despises and combats the old fashioned "history of events" or even biographical history, as some of it used to."[3]

I suspect there is more of a change than Hobsbawn, and perhaps even than Stone, admitted. The signs multiply that a major change is under way, one with important implications for all who are concerned with history. We are witnessing, I believe, not just a resurgent academic appreciation of some traditional techniques of historical scholarship, nor a recognition that narrative theory affects historical writing as much as it does the novel, but a rethinking of some of the fundamental modes whereby our culture relates to the past. The issue, if I am correct, is not just the revival of narrative but a new and more experiential mode of historical understanding. This large claim is not to be argued in short compass. My aim here is more modest, to look at one author from antiquity, writing in what I believe was a period similar in one respect to our own—its rethinking of its relationship to the past and of the problem of writing about the past. Studying narrative discourse in Thucydides will not by itself clarify what is happening in our own culture, but it may contain a few hidden analogies to some of the changes going on right now.

We have now almost stopped talking about Thucydides as a "scientific historian." That analogy, borrowed from the enthusiasms of an earlier generation, had a long life in Thucydidean studies and caused much belief. It encouraged the notion that Thucydides was not so much a writer as a proto-political scientist and sent readers scurrying about to find in his work "laws" comparable to those found by natural scientists. Much attention was thus paid to passages that generalized about human nature or that expounded the so-called Law of the Stronger. Little attention was paid to the fact that these passages are almost always found in the speeches of the work, and that the structure of the debates and their setting within the narrative often subvert or modify the generalizations advanced by individual speakers. The search for the laws of a political science in Thucydides made him into a hard line Cold Warrior, teaching the lesson of the tough-minded pursuit of self interest and national interest. The attempt to make

[3] E. Hobsbawm, "The Revival of Narrative: Some Comments," *Past and Present* 86 (1980) 3-8.

Thucydides into a "scientific historian," in other words, narrowed and distorted our understanding of the literary richness of the work. Still, the analogy did help us become aware of certain important features of the text, even if it did not go far toward explaining them. It drew attention to the restraint and austerity of Thucydides, the comparative infrequency of authorial interventions, and the avoidance of explicit judgments and evaluations. To be sure, it also tempted us to mistake these features for an attempt to write a purely "objective" or "value-free" history and to neglect the frequent and powerful indications of *implicit* value judgments throughout the *Histories*. The analogy to scientific history, in other words, did what analogies usually do — it opened our eyes to some features of the text and obscured some other features, equally important for a full and balanced appreciation.

Now that we have swung away from the view that Thucydides was a cold and detached observer and have begun to emphasize the elements of feeling, involvement, judgment, and pathos in his work, it is easy to be scornful of the old belief in a "scientific" Thucydides. But we learned a lot in that school, including the great debt Thucydides owed to the intellectual revolution of the mid fifth century B.C., especially to Hippocratic medicine and the early Sophists. Thucydides' work, we agree, was profoundly influenced — not molded or determined — but influenced by the thinking about myth, persuasion, and psychology that was going on during his childhood and youth. Out of that revolution Thucydides drew some of the elements that were to prove most important for his work. He combined a realistic, tough-minded psychology, the Hippocratics' insistence on careful testing of observations and reported facts, and the argumentative techniques of the Sophists into a powerful machine for historical analysis.

We can best see this engine at work in the opening chapters of the *Histories*, the so-called "Archaeology," where it is applied to the legends of early Greece. If we look closely, we note a surprising contrast between Thucydides and the supposedly more credulous Herodotus. Thucydides turns out to be willing to accept a considerable amount of this legendary material, but only after it has come through his analytical engine. Along the way the variants in the stories are studied, the alleged motives of the actors are tested against his "modern" psychology and an interpretation is presented that is grounded in analogies from primitive cultures and arguments from probability.

Consider one example. Herodotus begins his history of the Persian wars by telling some legends about early hostilities between Greeks and barbarians. He includes two versions of the story of Paris' abduction of Helen, but then dismisses both: "Which of these two accounts is true I shall not trouble to decide. I shall proceed at once to point out the person who first within my own knowledge commenced aggressions on the Greeks, after which I shall go forward with my history..." (Herodotus 1.5, trans. G. Rawlinson). Soon we are studying the expansions of the Persian empire in the sixth century B.C.

Thucydides, by contrast, refines and then accepts legends about early Greece. The opening of *his* history, the "Archaeology," accepts the reality of the Greek expedition against Troy. But he drastically reinterprets traditional legends: "Agamemnon," he says, "seems to me to have assembled his expedition not so much because of the oaths which Tyndareus imposed upon the suitors of Helen [that is, that they should assist the successful suitor if anyone ever abducted Helen] but because he was the most powerful man of his day" (1.9.1). He leaves no room here for story-telling about the power of oaths or the chivalric loyalty of unsuccessful suitors. Power counts and Agamemnon had it; naturally then, others followed when he gave the order. If we look through the *Histories* we find that Thucydides accepts a surprising amount of legendary material but accepts it only after his new historical method has separated plausible versions from myth, sentimentality and downright falsehood.

This method, Thucydides' new historical engine, is one of the boldest and most powerful inventions of the intellectual revolution of the fifth century. We understand it and appreciate it thanks in large part to the phase of our own past that emphasized the "scientific" nature of Thucydides' work. But that emphasis did little to help us understand how this historical method functions within the text. For that we must turn to the aspect of Thucydides that has attracted so much attention in recent years—the nature of narrative discourse. Much interesting work has been or is being done in this rich field, but I shall concentrate on a very specific question, and a very difficult one: Why do we believe Thucydides' account? What makes him seem so persuasive and compelling? To phrase the question in this way is not to imply that all historians believe Thucydides all the time—far from it. But those critics who have challenged Thucydides most sharply will be the first to point out the extraordinary hold he has upon our thinking about the Peloponnesian War. Even when his account has received repeated and serious criticism, historians and laymen alike are reluctant to repudiate it. To be sure we try to utilize *all* our sources about antiquity, especially those by contemporary writers, but Thucydides enjoys, rightly or wrongly, an esteem not accorded to Ctesias, Xenophon, Appian, Suetonius, or even Herodotus, Polybius, Livy and Tacitus. Why is this? The reason is not that Thucydides' account has been tested against a large number of independently verifiable facts and found consistently reliable. Only rarely can his work be compared to contemporary documents, and when it is compared, as when we have an inscription, there is almost always a problem. The problems do not *refute* Thucydides; we simply lack solid, independent verification. It is then something else that causes the intensity of belief engendered by Thucydides.

What is this something? Surely it is in part the recognition that Thucydides, whatever his biases and faults, is a highly intelligent observer. But how do we know that? And how can we test that impression? There is no sufficient outside authority to which we can appeal. We have only the words of the text to rely upon. In other words, the narrative discourse of Thucydides itself establishes the authority of the writer and persuades us to listen with respect, if not total assent.

It achieves this hold, moreover, without using many of the conventions of scholarly history. Obviously no one would expect to find in his work the apparatus of modern historical research, but the contrast between Thucydides and Herodotus indicates how rarely Thucydides uses the devices by which Herodotus presented to his readers the problems of finding out about the past. Herodotus will commonly identify the places where he finds a serious difficulty; he will report alternative versions or views; he will cite the consideration that leads him to prefer one version to another and he will state his conclusion in language that expresses the degree of confidence he feels. He may make mistakes of fact or logic; he may even be quite silly, but the problematic of history is always before our eyes. As Macan said in his appreciation of Herodotus in the *Cambridge Ancient History*, "Where there is a variant, he will not suppress alternatives, or impose his own judgment upon posterity. Even when his own mind is made up, he will allow his informants, and his public, the benefit of the doubt."[4] The historian and his reader are colleagues, sharing the problems and engaged in dialogue about their solution.

[4] R.W. Macan, *Cambridge Ancient History* Vol. 5 (Cambridge 1927) 414.

Thucydides' practice is quite the opposite. Through most of his work, he avoids discussing the problems of history and presents a finished product. As Macan says, "The results of his method, which is to extract for his readers, to all generations, a clear and chronologized narrative, the precise sources of which are seldom even indicated, must be taken or left on his authority, and on his authority alone."[5] Reader and author stand in a different relationship. They are not colleagues, but performer and audience, the writer who knows how to produce a polished work and the audience who appreciates its craftsmanship and reacts to its quality.

To Thucydides' detractors this is sufficient to condemn him for "brain-washing" or manipulation. We expect to be colleagues, especially if we are professional historians (not that Thudycides ever was), and feel cheated if we are not allowed to look over his shoulder at the reports and documents he is using. Thucydides' defenders, on the other hand, wax eloquent. Gomme, following Gilbert Murray, for example, wrote that Thucydides was "determined to do all the work himself and to present only the finished product to the public, as the artist does. Wren showed St. Paul's Cathedral to the world, not his plans for it; so does the painter his picture; so did Pheidias his sculpture."[6]

If we step aside for a moment from the speeches for the prosecution and the defense, we notice something that seems to me more important than praise or blame. Thucydides' avoidance or rejection of the conventions of historical argument make it all the more difficult to give a satisfactory answer to our original question: Why do we believe Thucydides? We do not believe him because he has identified and clarified the problems, cited his sources, gathered the evidence and established his conclusions with such plausibility that we are forced to assent. Perhaps we believe him for precisely the opposite reason — because he writes not as the scribes and Pharisees do, but with authority.

That authority derives, I believe, from three sources. To one I have already alluded: it is the demonstration of historical method in the "Archaeology." The opening twenty-three chapters are a short, highly selective inquiry into some aspects of the past and constitute an *epideixis*,

---

[5] Macan (above, note 4) 412.

[6] A.W. Gomme, *The Greek Attitude to Poetry and History* (Berkeley 1954) 119.

a demonstration piece, showing what Thucydides' method can do. They constitute an implicit *a fortiori* argument. If Thucydides' powerful engine can extract such a compelling interpretation of the remote past, *a fortiori* it should be able to attain important results in interpreting and analyzing the recent past. That, I believe, is what Thucydides implies when, after the investigation of early Greece, he points out the difficulties of finding out about the remote past but goes on to affirm that anyone who accepts the approximations he has derived from the indicators (*tekmēria*) he has mentioned will not go astray (1.21.1). He then turns to the problems of reconstructing the events of the Peloponnesian War. The famous "programmatic" or "methodological chapter" (1.22) is not a comprehensive statement of his historical principles but an affirmation of difficulties overcome and hence of the enduring utility of his work.

The first source of Thucydides' authority then is the demonstration of his historical method. But once the engine has been displayed, it is locked up again. We may hear it rumbling away in the background somewhere; we are reminded of its existence from time to time. But we do not regularly see it collecting, analyzing, testing and selecting reports and data about events and turning them into finished historical narrative.

Thus for much of the work the historical method of Thucydides is out of sight, if not entirely out of mind. In these portions its effects are reinforced by two further sources of authority. One is Thucydidean "style," that formidable, overwhelming complexity that can shatter all the neat antilogies and balances of Greek and strain the language to its limit.

Once again it is important to ask the simple but fundamental question. Why is Thucydides' style so difficult? Is it, as Collingwood thought, the result of Thucydides' bad conscience, his uneasiness at pretending to write history when he was really writing political science or theory?[7] Or is the more conventional answer correct—that it is the result of the originality and subtlety of his ideas. Is there some gnostic message concealed in the complexity of his expression? If we look closely, we find, I believe, that neither of these answers is correct. The difficulties derive not from the author's psychic disquiet nor from hidden subtleties, but from a desire to affirm his respect for the

[7] R. Collingwood, *The Idea of History* (New York 1956) 29.

complexity of historical events and human motives. In Thucydides we discover not an arcane philosophy but a style that replicates the intractability of historical experience. It assures the reader that the author will not oversimplify or reduce events to cliché, antithesis, or dogma.

This assurance is conveyed by, and much of the difficulty arises from, Thucydides' use of multiple viewpoints in narrating events. He will begin from one point of view, and switch, usually without warning or marker, to quite a different perspective. Often we end by viewing a single event from two or three different viewpoints. In the account of the third year of the war, for example, Thucydides tells of the consternation that swept through Athens when a Peloponnesian fleet appeared in the Saronic Gulf. The Peloponnesians had almost defeated the Athenian ships in the Corinthian Gulf. Then, at the end of the campaigning season, the Peloponnesian commanders decide to undertake one more operation. They will march their sailors overland, each carrying his oarlock and seat cushion, to Megara where forty ships are drawn up in their ally's dockyards. With these ships, they plan to make a surprise attack on the Piraeus.

Up to this point the narrative is straightforward, perfectly clear, even relatively easy Greek. Then follows a sentence of such contorted phraseology — not to mention its nine negatives in 35 words — that the critics have tried to emend it or delete it. Crawley's translation smooths out some of the difficulties but catches the main idea:

> There was no fleet on the look out in the harbor [of the Piraeus] and no one had the least idea of the enemy attempting a surprise: while an open attack would, it was thought, never be deliberately ventured on, or if in contemplation would be speedily known at Athens. (2.93.3)

Crawley has added a crucial phrase to the Greek: "while an open attack would, *it was thought*, never be deliberately ventured upon...". Why did Crawley add this phrase? He recognized and marked for his reader what is implicit and hence a source of obscurity in the Greek: that Thucydides has shifted from reporting the attitude of the Peloponnesians to conveying the psychology of the Athenians. In the next sentence, when Thucydides shifts back to the plans of the Peloponnesians, the reader understands, thanks to this contorted sentence, both the Peloponnesians' feeling that their original plan was terribly risky, and the ironic fact that precisely because of that risk it might well have worked:

...arriving at night and launching their vessels from Nisaea, they sailed, not to Piraeus as they originally intended, being afraid of the risk, besides which there was some talk of a wind having stopped them, but to the point of Salamis...

The rest of the account of the operation continues this alternation between Peloponnesian and Athenian viewpoints. The effect is consistently ironic: by the time we hear of the Peloponnesian decision to abandon their original plan we know that from the Athenian point of view it might have worked; by the time we hear of the panic in Athens, we know that from the Peloponnesian point of view the plan was too risky to carry through. The irony is characteristic of Thucydides and so are the rapid changes of viewpoint, a major component of his style and an important contributor to this second source of his authority.

The richness of Thucydides' account comes sharply into focus if we compare this passage to the smooth and nicely balanced version of the episode supplied by Diodorus of Sicily. Diodorus reduces all to a single viewpoint, that of one Peloponnesian commander; he omits the vivid detail of the march overland with each rower carrying his oarlock and seat cushion, and by failing to mention the growing fears of the Peloponnesian commanders leaves his reader without explanation for the outcome of the operation, an attack on Salamis not Piraeus:

In this year, Cnemus, the Lacedaemonian admiral, who was inactive in Corinth, decided to seize the Piraeus. He had received information that no ships in the harbour had been put into the water for duty and no soldiers had been detailed to guard the port; for the Athenians, as he had learned, had become negligent about guarding it because they by no means expected any enemy would have the audacity to seize the place. Consequently Cnemus, launching forty triremes which had been hauled up on the beach at Megara, sailed by night to Salamis, and falling unexpectedly on the fortress on Salamis called Boudorium, he towed away three ships and overran the entire island. (Diodorus 12.49.2-3, trans. C.H. Oldfather)

No one needs corroboration from contemporary documents or even a knowledge of the chronological and historiographical relationship between Thucydides and Diodorus to know which of these two accounts to prefer.

A third source of authority, however, may prove even more important. To call this the "experiential" or "participatory" aspect of

Thucydides' work would be cumbersome, but the terms for all their awkwardness call attention to a feature often neglected in the work. We do not usually think of Thucydides as a writer who keeps drawing his readers into the narrative of events until they feel they are themselves present, actually experiencing them. But Thucydides achieves this implication of the reader to an extraordinary degree. We do not often let ourselves be caught up in the vicarious experience of the actions he describes, but we should. For every minute we spend searching for laws or theory or gnostic insights, we might well allot equal time and attention to Thucydides' ability to recreate events and moods.

To achieve this end Thucydides has many techniques, chief among them the dramatic interplay between abstraction and sudden flashes of vividness. His style aspires to a level of generality that brings out the similarity of one episode to another. It often verges on the formulaic. But darting through it are words, phrases, sometimes whole episodes whose extraordinary vividness creates the illusion that we are ourselves present, witnessing events. In the passage we have just examined, for example, Thucydides notes that each sailor carried with him on the march his oarlock and cushion. In recounting the initial attack on Plataea, he focusses on the spear point jammed into the lock of the gate to prevent escape (2.4.3). At the siege of Plataea we observe the careful planning of the escape, the counting of the bricks (3.20.3), the removal of the sandal from the right foot (3.22.2), the armament and name of the leader of those who first climbed the ladders (3.22.3). In the account of the battle near Naupactus we watch an Athenian ship wheel rapidly about an anchored merchantman and ram its Leucadian pursuer amidship and sink it (2.91.3); on Sphacteria we experience the dust, the headgear pierced by arrows, the broken spears (4.34.3). Every attentive reader of Thucydides could expand the list and note the close bond between visual detail and the mood of the scene and the feelings of the participants. Vision in Thucydides is the privileged sense, most commonly invoked and most directly linked to the emotions.

Yet modern critics have said far less about the vivid side of Thucydides' style than about the complexities of his moral and political beliefs. In this respect, for all their obvious faults, the ancient critics are closer to the mark. Plutarch, for example, stressed Thucydides' use of *enargeia*, vividness, in his comments on Thucydides.

The most effective historian is the one who makes his narrative like a painting by giving a visual quality to the sufferings and characters. Thucydides certainly always strives after this vividness in his writing, eagerly trying to transform his reader into a spectator and to let the sufferings that were so dazzling and upsetting to those who beheld them have a similar effect on those who read about them. (Plutarch *On the Fame of the Athenians*, ch. 3 [*Moralia* 347A])

Hobbes made a similar observation, but set it in a more provocative context. He praised Thucydides as "the most politic historiographer that ever writ. The reason wherefore I take to be this... he maketh his auditor a spectator."[8] And how did Thucydides attain this most politic result? "The narrative," Hobbes says, "doth secretly instruct the reader and more effectively than can be done by precept." The political lessons and the utility of the *Histories*, in other words, derive not from Thucydides' explicit comments or implicit theorizing, but from the reader's own involvement in the work.

Once we recognize this, many features of the work become far more intelligible. We can worry less about the author's hidden theories and more about our own reactions to the text. And as we become more active participants in the events described, we can dispense with the narrator's guidance and explicit comments. The narrator can become self-effacing, speak in the the third person, intervene only rarely with his own judgments and evaluations and let the reader do, in Henry James' phrase, "quite half the labor." He may pretend that the war itself is the narrator which reveals its own greatness to those who scrutinize events closely enough (1.21.2).

We recognize, of course, that this *is* pretense, or a game in which reader and author engage. History is not chronicle, and Thucydides was certainly not a modest registering machine duly recording each event in colorless exactitude. He is present, selecting, shaping, coloring, at every episode, every phrase, every subscript. We ancient historians and philologists have reached the age of discretion at which we can reasonably be expected to recognize that the shaping of the text by the author, even as the author pretends to remove himself from his story, is not a bad habit, unprofessional conduct on the part of the writer. It is one way a writer can accomplish an essential part

---

[8] Thomas Hobbes, Preface to the translation of Thucydides (1629).

of his purpose—the involvement of the reader in the events and the activation of the reader's own evaluative capacities.

The illusion created by Thucydides, then, is one of immediate presence, of our own participation in the events described. That illusion, in Thucydides' view at least, excludes another one, and a very near and dear one to our historical hearts. Thucydides avoids letting his reader think that he is in the archive selecting the documents, or in the author's study participating in the choice of one version over another.[9] We are not his colleague. Instead, the documents have been gathered, the informants interrogated, the selection of alternative versions has been completed. This much of the work is done and the reader is presented with the final product and asked to respond to it.

In this respect Thucydides' practice contrasts very sharply with that of Herodotus. To many modern readers Herodotus is much more congenial. As we read his work we are constantly reminded of the difficulties he encountered in assembling and shaping his material—the legends and biased accounts presented to him as fact, the leg-pulling, the gaps and the polemics he encountered. We are at his side, sharing the decisions with him, and enjoying the process. By contrast Thucydides may seem to us, as he does to Truesdale Brown, to underestimate our intelligence:

> ...while breaking new ground in his scrupulous use of sources, he underestimated the intelligence of his readers. Having arrived at his own conclusions by a critical examination of the evidence he does not share the materials he rejects with the reader. Herodotus was less critical... he could not bear to omit anything which he felt might appeal to his readers.[10]

Brown's comments call attention to a major contrast between the two writers. But his explanation leaves out of sight the possibility that there are different principles at work. Thucydides imposes a different division of labor between author and reader. The historian's job is to investigate, compile, select, edit and present. The reader's half, the greater half, is to react, to assess, and thereby to learn.

This feature of Thucydides' technique has several important consequences for our understanding of the *Histories*, two of which call for special comment. The first concerns the ease with which description of mood is confused with statement of fact. The second returns

---

[9] One notable exception: 8.87.
[10] T.S. Brown, "Herodotus' Portrait of Cambyses," *Historia* 31 (1982) 402.

to the major topic of this paper, the establishment of Thucydides' authority.

First, mood. One of Thucydides' goals, we have suggested, was to create in his reader the illusion that he is himself present at events. Sometimes this goal leads to descriptions not of the event itself but of the reactions and feelings of those who were present at the event. The most famous of these passages is the description of the great naval battle in the harbor at Syracuse. The main portion of the description of the battle contains passages such as this:

> ...while the naval battle was hanging in the balance, the land army of each side experienced a great conflict and convergence of reactions. The group from the immediate area were eager to win, with a view to even greater glory; those who had invaded feared lest they should experience even worse than their present state. Since for the Athenians everything depended on the ships, their fear of the future was beyond any comparison and thanks to the uncertainty of the naval battle, uncertain too had to be the vision of it from the land. Since one could see only a small portion of the action, nor did all look at the same spot, those who saw in one engagement their own forces succeeding were encouraged and would turn to invocations of the gods not to deprive them of their safety. But those who looked at a defeat raised a ritual lament even while they were shouting and from the sight of what had happened lost their spirit even more than those who were in the engagement... (7.71.1-3)

The passage is an excellent example of several Thucydidean techniques — shifting viewpoints, the emphasis on vision, the creation of mood. But William Scott Ferguson deplored this approach:

> ...Thucydides fails even to suggest the factors that determined the outcome. Instead, he dwells on certain typical incidents in the confused fighting that followed, and then turns our attention to the spectators on the shore, and leaves us to infer the manifold vicissitudes of the protracted struggle from the agony of fear, joy, anxiety...

True enough. Thucydides' concern, however, was not to recover the tactics, such as they were, of this confused battle, but to record the changes in the morale of the Athenians, the crucial factor in the next stage of the operations. We have in this passage another kind of *enargeia*, a vividness not of precise details but of mood.

For the reader passages such as this pose special problems. One can, for example, mistake mood for fact. Again, Thucydides does not always stop to distinguish and to mark important differences. Sometimes it is not entirely clear whether he is telling us what the situation was or how it seemed to contemporary observers. At the beginning of book eight, for example, Thucydides discusses the situation in Athens when news came of the loss of the expedition in Sicily:

> All things on all sides grieved them and there surrounded them in this situation fear and dismay of the very greatest sort. For since they had lost, both individually and as a city, many heavy-armed soldiers and cavalry and crack troops of a quality the match of which they did not see to be available, they were depressed. Likewise since they did not see sufficient ships in their dockyards nor money in their treasury, nor crews for their ships, they despaired of any salvation in the present situation. They believed that the enemies from Sicily would immediately sail with their fleets against the Piraeus, especially since they had conquered so decisively, and that their own more immediate enemies at that very time had made double efforts in full force and would bear down upon them from land and sea and that their own allies would revolt and join them. (8.1.2-3)

The passage tells us how the Athenians looked upon their situation in the bleak moments when the news about Sicily arrived. It is full of descriptions of feelings — how they saw things, what they *believed* would happen. But many excellent commentators take the passage as Thucydides' assertion of *facts*, and then point out, using evidence from other passages in Thucydides, that the situation was by no means as hopeless as this passage suggests. Meiggs, for example, writes "the empire, meanwhile, according to Thucydides, threatened collapse as the allies competed fiercely to be the first to revolt, now that Athens' power was broken. His detailed narrative does not fully bear out this gloomy analysis."[11] And Andrewes in the new Oxford commentary on book eight (p.6), noting that Athenian despair about their navy, concludes, "clearly the decree of 431 (ii.24.2) had not been maintained to keep a reserve of a hundred triremes, the best of each year, in readiness with their trierarchs." Perhaps not, but as Andrewes points out, their despair about their finances makes no mention of the reserve fund of one thousand talents also established in 431 and still available for use in the post-Sicilian emergency (8.15.1). Thucydides says that the Athenians did not *see* the resources to deal with the present situation; he does not say there were no resources to see.

[11] R. Meiggs, *The Athenian Empire* (Oxford 1972) 351.

As we read on in book eight the facts gradually become clear and the mood of the Athenians gradually changes: there *is* a reserve fund; not *all* allies revolt; those that do revolt often act prematurely; Sparta is not effective in exploiting the situation and the Syracusans are not swift or decisive in their intervention. At Cynossema Athens wins a major victory. In the eighth book we trace an irregular movement from despair to growing confidence, from apparent defeat to the renewed efforts of the Athenians in a final, and even greater, struggle. If we understand Thucydides' emphasis on changing moods, this book becomes more intelligible and we are far less likely, here or elsewhere, to mistake description of moods for statements about facts.

In a second way too we can now better understand Thucydides' technique and why it has produced such intense conviction. At certain points the narrative creates in the reader the feeling of being directly present at an episode in the war. We are as far from the historians' study as we can possibly be; we are in the war itself. We see; we hear; we even know the plans and thoughts of the participants. The crucial elements are before us, not in pictorial fullness, as one might find in a Hellenistic historian, but through highly selective detail. As Lawrence Stone has said of Peter Brown, "The deliberate vagueness, the pictorial approach,... the concern for what was going on inside people's heads, are all characteristic of a fresh way of writing history."[12] And like a *pointilliste* painting it draws us in, involves our minds in the process of creation, and wins our assent. Seeing is, after all, believing.

Those who have learned what history is from professional scholars and who know a good footnote when they see one, may find this a paradoxical conclusion. How can one believe a writer who, after a few opening chapters, simply bypasses the whole problematic of history and writes as if he knew precisely what went on in the war, and even in the participants' heads? If we had been weaned on Macaulay and Carlyle, things might look different. Those writers remind us that in History's house there are many rooms and many passageways. We lose something if we block off too many parts of the mansion or condemn too much of it too soon.

And what is it, precisely, we risk if we close the chambers Thucydides occupied? The loss of vicarious experience and of the sense of participating in a reality far different from our daily life, the very

---

[12] Stone (above, note 1) 17.

thing that makes the study of history so important for the growth of the mind and imagination. "But surely," one might object, "this vicarious experience can be obtained without sacrificing the constant gestures of respect for the problematic of history which are the marks of modern scholarly history." Perhaps, but one should not underestimate the difficulty. For many readers any pause over the problems of historical evidence and reconstruction, any worry about conflicting sources or assessments, any entry into the historian's study, shatters the illusion of participating in the past. The problematic of history impedes its experiential power. To talk about the problems of historical analysis imposes a chasm between reader and past event. Even when it produces conviction, a residue of doubt remains. For historical analysis is always based on the calculation of probabilities. We read the arguments and assent, but our language reminds us of the uncertainty. We say we are "almost one hundred percent sure" or that we are "halfway convinced" or that we have "found the preponderance of evidence" on one side of the matter.

The division of labor we have noted in Thucydides bypasses this problem. Thucydides may have his doubts and unresolved problems. But he keeps them to himself and lets the reader transcend them. The conviction which attends the reading of Thucydides' work is thus not related to the calculation of probabilities or the careful assessment of plausible solutions. We feel we have been there. The world Thucydides has described, the patterns of power and human conduct, are so consistent, so real, that we have no choice but to assent. We are moved by the greater logic that derives its power not from ac-cumulated evidence or carefully constructed syllogisms but from the evocation of a coherent world. At length we feel, not that we have deduced the nature of that world, but that we have temporarily become part of it. Of course we then believe — not despite, but because of the fact that Thucydides does not write as the scribes and Pharisees do, but as one with authority.

What shall we then conclude about Thucydides' authority? Why *do* we believe him? We have seen three sources of it in the work, the first the powerful engine of historical analysis whose workings are best to be seen in the "Archaeology." The second is a style that affirms the author's respect for the complexity of historical events and that views the past from multiple perspectives. The third source, perhaps the most important, is the reader's feeling of experiencing the events described.

The sources do not all cohabit in blissful harmony. Indeed between the second and the third there is an inevitable tension—the rapid shifting of viewpoints risks a shattering of the experiential quality of the work. But Thucydides' style not only contributes to his authority but sustains the tension and transforms it into the uniquely powerful result we have all experienced in reading Thucydides. It accounts for something scholars of Thucydides experience but often fail to mention—Thucydides' appeal as a writer and the pleasure of reading him. If we concentrate too much on the scientist or philosopher, we lose sight of the vividness of his writing and the rich, demanding but rewarding experience of reading a great writer. Expecting profundity we can miss the color, the swift-paced action, the detail, the opportunity to see, to experience, to understand. To say this is not to make Thucydides into a simple writer, not to minimize the efforts he expects from his readers. But it is a reminder of the ability of this work to avoid the eventual emptiness of an exclusively analytical method and to resist with equal determination the tendency so evident in Hellenistic historiography to report anything that is sufficiently lurid and sensational. What makes Thucydides' work what it is— one of the unsurpassed and enduring achievements of prose narrative—is precisely this tension and interaction among different modes of narrative discourse.

Why Do We Believe Thucydides? A Comment on W.R. Connor's "Narrative Discourse in Thucydides"

PAUL ROBINSON
Stanford University

Professor Connor has addressed the question, "Why do we believe Thucydides? Why does his account of the Peloponnesian War command assent?" And I think I should begin by noting that the question, at least in this form, strikes me as somewhat oppressive, since it takes for granted that we *do* in fact believe him. In truth, however, some people don't find Thucydides especially believable. R.G. Collingwood, for example, wrote in *The Idea of History* as if he considered *The Peloponnesian War* incredible from first word to last.

A less tendentious version of Professor Connor's question, then, might run, "Why do we believe Thucydides when we *do* believe him?" This formulation has the virtue of letting us off the hook when we come to those passages of the history — and they are among its most famous — that don't boast the same persuasiveness as do the more strictly narrative passages to which Professor Connor draws our attention. I am thinking especially of the great "set pieces" of the work: the Congress at Sparta, with its stylized discussion between Corinthians and Athenians about the logic of imperialism; the systematic analysis of the biology and psychology of the plague in Book Two; the so-called "Mytilene Debate," with its subtle exploration of the rationale of punishment; and, finally, the "Melian Dialogue" of Book Five, which

19

is, in effect, a dialectical treatise on the psychology of war and the purposes of military conquest. Exactly these passages, of course, have given rise to the contention that Thucydides was less a historian than a political scientist or even a political philosopher. Perhaps significantly, none of them figures in Professor Connor's analysis.

Let me turn, therefore, to the three sources of Thucydides' persuasiveness that Professor Connor discusses. I would like, if I might, to take them up in reverse order.

I. First there is the proposition that we believe Thucydides because of his vividness — because he gives the reader a sense of being present at the events described. Professor Connor contrasts this tactic of persuasion — indeed, contrasts it invidiously — with that of the archival historian who allows us to watch him examining the sources and weighing the virtues of alternative accounts. In other words, he contrasts Thucydides' tactic with that of Herodotus.

In mounting his argument, Professor Connor adduces the authority of Plutarch and Hobbes, both of whom comment on the visual or pictorial quality of Thucydides' history, and both of whom explicitly associate that quality with his credibility. Plutarch says that the most effective historian, such as Thucydides, "makes his narrative like a painting by giving a visual quality to the sufferings and characters," while Hobbes says that Thucydides "maketh his auditor a spectator."

I find these assertions somewhat puzzling, although my difficulty may stem from an overliteral sense of what one means by "visual" or what's entailed in being a "spectator." If one simply means that the narrative is "life-like" (the word Professor Connor uses most often is "vivid"), then I see no particular problem. On the other hand, I do not find Thucydides a notably pictorial writer in the strict sense of bringing visual images to mind. Professor Connor writes that "vision in Thucydides is the privileged sense," and that may well be the case. But much of what is most important in Thucydides transpires beneath (or perhaps beyond) the level of sense experience, visual or otherwise. In particular his preoccupation with psychology works very strongly *against* a visual mode of absorption, and, indeed, many of the passages that Professor Connor cites in his paper deal, as he himself notes, with what goes on inside people's heads. Of course, what goes on inside people's heads may be vividly rendered — and Thucydides certainly achieves just such psychological vividness — but since those processes are largely invisible, it seems rather awkward to characterize their representation as "pictorial" or "visual."

This, however, is something of a quibble or a matter of terminological confusion. A more serious issue pertains to the assumption that Thucydides' tactic of experiential history is in fact more persuasive than the archival or pharisaic tactic of Herodotus (and, in Professor Connor's opinion, of most modern historians as well). I would suggest, on the contrary, that the relative persuasiveness of these two approaches varies considerably from one reader to the next: some of us are more convinced by the "you-are-there" approach, others of us by being taken into the author's confidence. Moreover, I rather suspect that the archival tactic gains in credibility as readers become more sophisticated.

In any case, if vividness or the sense of actually being there is the main source of Thucydides' ability to persuade, I don't see how one can easily distinguish his performance from that of a novelist, who also deludes us into believing that we are live witnesses to the events portrayed in his book. After we have finished the novel, however, our sense of the reality of those events is quite different from what it was during the actual process of reading. And if that is so, what is to prevent us from feeling the same way about Thucydides after we have laid *his* book aside? In other words, if he persuades us by vividness, then is there not reason to worry about the durability of his claim on our convictions? I note in this context that Professor Connor several times refers to the *illusion* Thucydides creates of our being present at the purported events. Well, if Professor Connor has been able to detect that this creation is only illusory, then he has for all practical purposes undermined the source of his own confidence in the text's authority. He is not quite the naive reader that he yearns to be or that he imagines as Thucydides' ideal audience.

II. Professor Connor also proposes that Thucydides' prose style is among the important sources of his ability to make us believe. The salient quality of that prose style, he suggests, is its complexity, which persuades us because it reflects the complexity of the real world as we experience it.

The observation is incontrovertible. I would only warn against what might be called "the pathos of complexity." When I was in graduate school in the 1960s, the highest compliment we could pay anyone was to say of that person, "He's very complex." Being complex was even better than being intelligent, not to mention being virtuous. But if carried to extremes—especially in the matter of prose style—the pathos of complexity can lead to results exactly contrary to those Professor

Connor associates with the quality. Instead of producing an immediate sense of believability, it in fact elicits just the opposite: it requires of the reader a sustained and systematic effort to suspend disbelief. Two writers who are victims of the pathos of complexity are Hegel and Michel Foucault, and I would suggest that in reading Hegel or Foucault our response is very different from our response to Thucydides. We are always on the verge of saying, "This is all nonsense, I don't believe a word of it" — or, perhaps more likely — "I don't *understand* a word of it," and we persist in reading such works not because of but in spite of their complexity.

My caveat is in a sense gratuitous, since, as already noted, Thucydides suffers from no such proclivity. As Professor Connor lets us see, Thucydides is complex only when the occasion calls for it, and he also knows how to be simple. Thus that extraordinarily involuted sentence with its nine negatives, whose psychological nuances Professor Connor skilfully decodes for us, is mercifully preceded by a narrative that, in Professor Connor's own words, is "straightforward, perfectly clear, even relatively easy." This judicious balance of the straightforward and the complex ought to be a model for all historians, and I fully agree that it is an important source of Thucydides' credibility.

III. Finally, Professor Connor writes that we believe Thucydides because he is so manifestly intelligent. I find this the most interesting, and yet also most paradoxical, of the three sources to which he attributes Thucydides' ability to persuade.

I should say at once that I am entirely in accord with the estimation of Thucydides' intelligence. Indeed, I think he may be the smartest historian I have ever read. And Professor Connor is surely right to argue that the opening chapters of the history, the so-called "Archaeology," serve primarily to convince us of just how smart he really was. These chapters are almost acrobatic in their display of intellectual power. When I first read them I had the sense that I was witnessing one of the great moments in the emergence of Western man's critical faculties.

But let me be slightly perverse and suggest that Thucydides may have been *too* smart — or at least too smart to be a historian. I am rather fond of the notion that historians need a certain capacity for stupidity. Henry Thomas Buckle seems to have shared my opinion, since he wrote: "Any author who from indolence of thought, or from natural incapacity, is unfit to deal with the highest branches of knowledge, has only to pass some years in reading a certain number of books, and then he is qualified to be an historian." Historians need a tolerance for stupidity precisely for the reason that they need a tolerance for complexity: because human reality, just as it is sometimes complex, is also sometimes embarrassingly stupid.

From this perspective one might argue that exactly those parts of Thucydides' history that many have found unconvincing are unconvincing because in them he tries to impose a kind of orderliness onto human affairs that is quite foreign to the dumb, intractable disorder of real life. These are the famous passages that I mentioned earlier on, the great set pieces, in which he dons the mantle of political philosopher. They are also, of course, the very passages that so annoyed R.G. Collingwood and led him to assert that Thucydides was not a historian at all. In them, we sometimes feel, Thucydides has created reality after the image of his own mind, and, as a result, we don't believe him.

So intelligence, I would suggest, is a double-edged sword as far as a historian's credibility is concerned. To be sure, we are more inclined to believe someone if we're convinced that the person is smart, but when smartness leads to alienation from the untidiness of history and to an effort to refashion it after the mind's own categories, then the historian ceases to persuade. And from time to time, it seems to me, Thucydides undeniably falls victim to this temptation. He may be the greater thinker for having so yielded, but he is perhaps the lesser historian.

Epigrams and History: The Athenian Tyrannicides, A Case in Point

JOSEPH W. DAY
Wabash College

One of our motivations for analyzing the works of the ancient historians as self-conscious literary creations is the desire to determine to what extent, and for what purposes, those authors distorted "the whole truth" by omitting or amplifying what we might wish they had simply recorded.[1] No one will deny that the distorting process of selection can serve the higher purposes of factual accuracy, historical interpretation, and literary merit. Thucydides' version of Perikles' *Epitaphios*, for example, remains a brilliant exposé of the cultural ideals of fifth-century Athens, and Perikles may even have voiced the sentiments attributed to him by the historian. Still, we have to ask

[1] For the references used throughout this paper, see the Bibliography. I am grateful to Profs. J.A.K. Anderson, L.P. Day, D.R. Laing, D.M. Lewis, W.B. Stanford, A. Stewart, M.B. Walbank, M.B. Wallace, and D.C. Young for comments, criticisms, and responses to inquiries. They are of course in no way responsible for omissions, inaccuracies, and unfounded speculations in the text that follows. Thanks are also due to the Greek Archaeological Service and the local ephor, Mr. Ilias Tsiribakos, for permission to examine the Chian stone discussed below. I should also like to thank the College of Wooster for partially funding my travel in Greece in 1982 and the American School of Classical Studies at Athens for the use of its facilities. Finally, I join my colleagues in expressing profound gratitude and sincerest congratulations to Professor Raubitschek.

25

ourselves to what extent his speech mirrors the way Athenians generally thought and spoke about their city. Other extant funeral orations,
as well as other literature and non-literary sources, suggest that Athenian audiences demanded a far less idealistic and more crudely emotional version of their city's past and its current nature; and the orators
acceded to this demand by trotting out bits of a conventional body
of patriotic lore which, when taken together, could be said to constitute a tradition of Athenian history. If we could explicate such conventional views of history, we would certainly add to our understanding of Athenian society. More important in the context of this volume,
however, such knowledge might enable us to read the literary historians
with new insights into their reasons for selecting and interpreting the
way they did.

A considerable body of scholarship has taken as its subject the relationship between the literary histories and what Athenians generally
believed, or what we might call "popular traditions of history."[2] Partly because this relationship is an important one, but also because we
owe to Antony E. Raubitschek and his colleague at Stanford, Lionel
Pearson, much of the best work on this topic, I hope that I may be
forgiven in what follows for straying from the literary historians to
a popular tradition.

Another of the great students of popular traditions, Felix Jacoby,
employed as a test case for his analysis the tradition about the murder
of Hipparchos.[3] This Hipparchos was, of course, the son of the Athenian tyrant Peisistratos; he was murdered in 514 B.C. by two men
of the clan of the Gephyraioi, Harmodios and Aristogeiton. The story
of his murder is told briefly by Herodotus, in some detail by
Thucydides, and in even more detail by Aristotle in his *Constitution
of the Athenians*.[4] In spite of some scholarly disagreement, it is fair to
say that these three authors essentially agree both about the facts and
their proper interpretation. They also agree in their tone, which is
polemical, and the polemic is most pronounced in Thucydides, who
aims it directly at a rival version of the events and their significance.

---

[2] The question of whether one should speak of "traditions" or "a tradition" remains
unresolved. In *The Glory of Athens* (Chicago 1980), I argue for a high degree of consistency in popular versions of at least one phase of fifth-century Athenian history.
[3] *Atthis* (Oxford 1949), Chapter III, 2, "The Tradition about the Peisistratids,"
152-168.
[4] Hdt. 5.55-65; Thuc. 1.20.2; 6.53.3-60.1; *Ath. Pol.* 17.2-19.1.

Jacoby suggests — and he may be right — that Thucydides was reacting specifically to the account of Hellanikos, whose Attic history had come out a few years before Thucydides' own work. However, Thucydides makes it clear that the rival version was much more than one man's written account; it was what τὸ πλῆθος 'Αθηναίων believed, and they believed it because it was what they had always heard (Thucydides' word is ἀκοή) and because it was emotionally attractive.[5] In the narratives of the murder of Hipparchos, then, we may well have access to a genuine popular tradition; that is, a version of historical events that was generally accepted by the Athenians of Thucydides' day.

When we try to reconstruct this popular tradition, we have to deal with two kinds of sources, each presenting its own peculiar problem. First, there are the historians. Since their accounts are at least partly polemical, we have to be prepared to argue in reverse. For example, if Thucydides, in very polemical passages, argues that the tyranny was good before 514, that Hipparchos did not hold an official position, and that the murder was not a very effective act, then we should probably conclude that in the popular tradition the tyranny was evil before 514, Hipparchos was an important officer, and the assassination was an extremely significant act. Jacoby, in fact, believed that this tradition incorrectly synchronized the assassination of 514 with the liberation of Athens from tyranny in 510. He further argued that this popular version originated in oral, family stories that were put to work in propaganda battles among the noble families soon after the liberation.[6]

The second type of source is just as slippery as the first, but slippery in a very different way. These are the sources for the story of Harmodios and Aristogeiton as it was transmitted outside the historians. The evidence includes:

1. A statuary group, now lost, of Harmodios and Aristogeiton. It was executed by Antenor and erected at public expense in the Athenian Agora sometime between 510 and 480, when it was carried off

---

[5] This attractiveness is evidenced by the many popular sources listed below, but Thucydides himself seems to comment on it by juxtaposing 1. 20 and 21. Moreover, his longer excursus in 6 begins from a mention of the emotional power the story held among the Athenians of his day (53.3).

[6] Jacoby saw this version as anti-Alkmaionid. V. Ehrenberg, "Origins of Democracy," *Historia* 1 (1950) 515-548; "Das Harmodioslied," *WS* 69 (1956) 57-69, saw it as pro-Alkmaionid.

to Persia by Xerxes. The base may have been inscribed with an epigram.[7]

2. A replacement group by Kritios and Nesiotes, erected in 477, probably with an epigram. The original is lost, but the many fragments of Roman copies seem to imitate this one rather than that of Antenor.[8]

3. The bestowal of special civic rights and privileges upon the descendants of Harmodios and Aristogeiton.[9]

4. A set of four skolia praising the deed of Harmodios and Aristogeiton. These may be quite early, even from before 510.[10]

5. A publicly sanctioned grave of the tyrannicides in the *demosion sema*.[11]

6. A hero-cult, with annual *enagismata*, in honor of the tyrannicides.[12]

There are serious problems involved in interpreting this material, but two considerations make the effort well worthwhile. First, clearly some, perhaps all, of these testimonia reflect publicly sanctioned attitudes older than any of the literary histories. Second, each of them could further be interpreted as a genuine instrument for the expression of broadly based, popular sentiment.

Needless to say, the scholarly debate on the popular tradition about the murder of Hipparchos is immense.[13] Fortunately, I am concerned here with only one detail in this debate, namely, the text of any epigram or epigrams inscribed on the base of either the Antenor or the later statuary group. For this purpose I have found the most sensible and helpful analysis of the literary sources to be that contained in a pair

---

[7] For the best summaries of the ancient evidence, cf. Taylor, especially the lists on 198-209, and S. Brunnsåker, *The Tyrant-Slayers of Kritios and Nesiotes: A Critical Study of the Sources and Restorations*[2] (Stockholm 1971).

[8] *Ibid.*

[9] *IG* I[2], 77 = I[3], 131; cf. Isae. 5. 47; Plut. *Ar.* 27. 6; M. Ostwald, "The Prytaneion Decree Re-examined," *AJP* 72 (1951) 24-46; Fornara 1970, 169, n. 59.

[10] Cited by Ath. 15. 695; nos. 893-896 in D.L. Page, *Poetae Melici Graeci* (Oxford 1962). For ancient allusions and references to these songs, cf. Taylor 203. For recent treatments, cf. Taylor 51-71; M. Ostwald, *Nomos and the Beginnings of the Athenian Democracy* (Oxford 1969) 121-137.

[11] Paus. 1.29.15.

[12] Arist. *Ath.Pol.* 58.1.

[13] Cf. the comments of Fornara 1968, 400 and n. 1.

of articles by Charles Fornara.[14] Among the many points Professor Fornara makes, four seem to have special value for a study of the epigram(s). First, we ought not to follow Jacoby in overemphasizing the nature of the popular tradition as "official" in the sense that it represented a program of propaganda. We must recognize it as a true "vulgate" tradition that was popularly believed at least partly because of the fact that it was somehow attractive to people in general. Perhaps it was "dramatic" or in some other way appealed to the emotions of the general public.[15] Second, those who stress the tyrannicide cult as an element of political propaganda make a serious error in maintaining that the popular tradition identified Harmodios and Aristogeiton as the liberators of 510 B.C.[16] Since Thucydides did not direct his polemic against such a misconception, it must not have existed in the tradition to his time; in fact, he shows that the Athenians knew perfectly well that it was the Spartans who freed Athens in that year. Third, the expectation that a true tyrannicide should "act out of political or ideological considerations" was in fact the assumption of Thucydides. The early tradition was not concerned with ideology or constitutional niceties, but rather with the act of Harmodios and Aristogeiton, which served as τιμωρία for the ὕβρις of the tyrant and was sealed as a heroic deed by their noble death.[17] That the liberation and eventually the establishment of the democracy were associated indirectly with the tyrannicides, and that they became heroes of the new government, cannot be denied; but in the early tradition it was the deed and death of the men that were most dramatic and attractive and elevated those men to the level of Homeric heroes. Finally, Fornara says that more attention needs to be paid to the earliest stages of the tradition, that is, the skolia and especially the statuary group by Antenor and any early epigram.[18] It is to the epigrams that we must now turn.

---

[14] 1968, 1970.

[15] Fornara 1970, 169f. One might, in the manner of G. Nagy, *The Best of the Achaeans* (Baltimore and London 1979), 174f., distinguish cultic testimonia (*e.g.*, the second skolion) from those which depend on the χάρις of art or poetry to grant eternal κλέος.

[16] Jacoby (above, note 3) 342f., n. 73, based on the notion that this tradition was in Hellanikos, who is thus accurately summarized at *Marmor Parium*, A, ep. 45. Cf. Fornara 1970, 162 and 171.

[17] Fornara 1968, 405.

[18] Fornara 1970, 158, n. 23, disagrees with Podlecki 1966, who concentrates only on the later statuary group. Fornara also argues against the downdating of Antenor's group to "not before 487" by Raubitschek, 481-483, 513-516.

One can say, without creating a straw man, that there is a *communis opinio* concerning the evidence for the inscriptions on the bases of the tyrannicide groups that stood in the Agora.[19] It consists in two tenets, with a third frequently appended. First, the inscribed fragment found in the Agora in 1936 carries the ends of two elegiac distichs and comes from the base of the Kritios-Nesiotes monument of 477.[20] It reads:

]ḥαρμοδιο[
πα]τρίδα γε̃ν ἐθέτεν.

Second, the proper restoration of the first distich should depend on the two lines quoted by Hephaistion in his *Encheiridion*, where they are ascribed to Simonides, ἐκ τῶν ἐπιγραμμάτων:[21]

ἦ μέγ' 'Αθηναίοισι φόως γένεθ', ἡνίκ' 'Αριστο-
γείτων 'Ίππαρχον κτεῖνε καὶ 'Αρμόδιος.

Hephaistion was interested in the poet's handling of Aristogeiton's name, which presumably explains why the second distich was omitted. Third, this epigram was probably copied verbatim from the one on the base of the Antenor group.[22]

Many investigators, myself included, have been drawn at least to the first two tenets of this consensus, not only because they explain the evidence plausibly, but also because they make good aesthetic sense. Hephaistion's lines are really quite good and certainly worthy of Simonides.[23] And I wish to stress that, even in the face of the kind of scholarly objections that will be brought forward in the following pages, one must allow that a poet of Simonides' caliber is always capable of composing something surprising. Moreover, Hephaistion's couplet seems to complement the aesthetic impact of the generally

[19] The most serious challenges to the *opinio* would come from those who with Raubitschek would downdate the Antenor group so far that the Agora fragment could be assigned to it, or those who would argue that the fragment itself is older than is regularly allowed (so Prof. M.B. Walbank, privately).

[20] Meritt; *SEG* 10.320.

[21] *Ench.* 4.6. The poem is also cited by Eust. *Il.* 984.8. The latest treatments appear at Hansen no. 430 and Page 186-189.

[22] Meritt 358. This is accepted, with a caveat, by P. Friedländer and H. Hoffleit, *Epigrammata* (Berkeley and Los Angeles 1948) 141f.; cf. Jacoby (above, note 3) 339, n. 52. It is opposed by Podlecki 1966, 136f.; Page 188.

[23] The best literary commentary on the poem is still that of Friedländer.

accepted reconstructions of the statues by Kritios and Nesiotes. The highly emotional emphasis on the single dramatic moment which, in its well-known significance, recalls to the viewer-reader the whole narrative and its meaning — this "stop action" technique — seems obvious in both poem and statues.[24]

Thus, it is without a preconceived desire to disprove Hephaistion's couplet as a genuine, early tyrannicide epigram that I raise two issues which in fact do cast this poem's authenticity into doubt. First, the poem seems to exhibit the kind of anachronistic ideologizing against which Fornara warned. Friedländer correctly interprets the dramatic opening, ἦ μέγ' Ἀθηναίοισι φόως γένετο, as a ringing announcement of the liberation of Athens from tyranny.[25] He maintains that for the composer of these lines the liberation was most important, not the act of assassination, which was placed in the subordinate construction. Furthermore, if this couplet were followed by another whose end appears on the Agora fragment, it would seem that the poem must end, as well as begin, with a political statement. The pentameter would likely conclude with ἰσόνομον πα]τρίδα γἔν (Peek), or ἐν ἐλευθερίᾳ πα]τρίδα γἔν (Friedländer), or something of the sort. Hence, even if we are faced with a lacuna of over one verse, we shall be reasonably secure in maintaining that the poem gave priority to Athens' liberation from tyranny as a direct political result of the murder of Hipparchos. Thus, the composer identified the tyrannicide and the liberation in just the way that Fornara argues did not exist in the popular tradition before Thucydides.

My second objection stems from problems about the typology of both the monument and our putative epigram and about the relationship between the two.[26] Some, including Meritt, have called this

---

[24] Cf. Friedländer 90f. I have borrowed the term "stop action" from J.J. Pollitt's treatment in the *Fest* for Prof. Cedric Boulter, University of Cincinnati, April 2, 1982. The Greek is ῥυθμός, for which cf. Pollitt, *The Ancient View of Greek Art* (New Haven and London 1974) 218-228.

[25] Friedländer 90f., who, for example, points out that φόως can bear the metaphorical meaning of "rescue" in Homer; cf. *Il.* 11.797. Also cf. the imagery of the *Oresteia*, esp. *Choeph.* 863.

[26] In this and the following paragraphs, discussion of the statues must be limited to the group by Kritios and Nesiotes. Our knowledge of Antenor's group is very limited; hypotheses range from two late-archaic kouros figures to the prototypes for the later group; cf. M. Robertson, *A History of Greek Art* (Cambridge 1975) I 186. This problem, however, may have little or no bearing on the present issue, since

poem dedicatory.[27] Friedländer was more careful. He pointed out that the statues were not gods, canonical heroes, grave figures, or dedications, and he noted that the poem does not exhibit the formal characteristics of any traditional type—funerary, votive, etc.[28] Friedländer argued that we have here a new type of poem for a new type of monument, a "national-political monument." In a sense that we shall examine below, he was correct about this monument's newness; but he failed to define what his new type of poem was and he could not bring forward convincing parallels, since other epigrams on early public monuments of the democracy are all close to a traditional type, epitaph or dedication. Moreover, Friedländer and others have failed to consider the extent to which the monuments mounted on the bases, together with any prose inscriptions, predominated over the epigrams in importance. Although the epigrams might appear to us to contain information essential to the viewer's appreciation of the monument, the Greeks' highly developed sense of folk memory probably rendered the epigram much less essential to ancient viewers. They would have known the major monuments of their cities and the popular tradition about each monument. They might even have known snippets of longer poems composed to celebrate the same event as the monument did and perhaps alluded to in the epigram itself. Hence, the epigrams must be considered, in an important sense, decorative additions to the monuments, and this attitude is precisely what one finds confirmed in three famous epigrams of the period.[29] Each poem contains a single, major idea that closely reflects or comments on the monument itself; other thoughts, causes, results, narratives, etc., are subordinated to this one comment, even though they may seem vital in themselves.

The first two examples clearly illustrate my point, in spite of their troublesome lacunae (Hansen 2.ii and 2.iii):

---

in all likelihood both groups could be said to have served the same purpose; hence, I use the apparently ambiguous term "monument." Later, where the viewer's emotional reaction to the monument is discussed, I again have the later group in mind; but there, since any differences between the groups could be important, the reader is urged to beware.

[27] Meritt 356, n. 2; Podlecki 1966, 135.

[28] Friedländer 90.

[29] All texts are those of Hansen, who reviews the bibliographies and major problems.

(i) ἀνδρõν τõνδ᾽ ἀρετε͂[ς ?ἔσται κλέ]ˌος ἄφθιˌ[τον] αἰεί :
    [....9....]ν[.]ρ[..ca. 7..]ˌνέμοσι θεοίˌ · |
    ἔσχον γὰρ πεζοί τε [καὶ] ˌὀκυπόρον ἐπὶ νεõˌν :
    ℎελλά[δα μ]ὲ πᾶσαν δούλιοˌν ἔμαρ ἰδε͂νˌ.

(ii) ἐν ἄρα τοῖσζ᾽ ἀδαμ[α ‿‿ _ ‿‿ _ ‿] ℎότ᾽ αἰχμὲν
    στε͂σαμ πρόσθε πυλõν ἀγ[‿ ‿ _ ‿ ‿ _] |
    ἀνχίαλομ πρε͂σαι ρ̣[‿‿ _ ‿‿ ‿‿‿ _]ο
    ἄστυ βίαι Περσõν κλινάμενο[ι ‿ ‿ _].

Both epigrams begin by pointing to the monument(s) for which they were composed, apparently casualty lists or something else referring to Athenian troops (τõνδ᾽, τοῖσζ᾽). The structure and perhaps also the sentiment of each initial verse are similar to those of the other and reflect the form of an epitaph.[30] The first verse of (i) at least is related to the monument in a further way: the men's glory will last as long as the names on the monument are remembered. This sentiment of longevity may well be continued in the second verse of (i), but the rest of (i), although important, serves structurally to explain (γάρ) the reason for the thoughts in the first distich and thus the reason for the monument's erection. Apparently everything after ℎότ᾽ in (ii) is not only explanatory but also grammatically subordinated; thus, it all functions similarly to the second distich of (i).

The third epigram appears to present a problem (Hansen 179):

(iii) ˌδεσμõι ἐν †ἀχλυόεντι† σιδερέοι ἔσβεσαν ℎύβˌρινꞏ
    παῖδεˌς ᾽Αθηναίον ἔργμασιν ἐμ πολέμοˌ |
    ˌἔθνεα Βοιοτõν καὶ Χαλκιδέον δαμάσαντεςˌ,꞉
    τõν ℎίππος δˌεκάτεν Παλλάδι τάσδ᾽ ἔθεσανˌ.

The first verse looks as though it records, without reference to the monument, the kind of explanation that was secondary in the examples above; yet it is not subordinated and appears to be parallel to the last verse, the traditional formula of dedication with the requisite reference to the monument. In fact, however, the information about iron fetters reminds us "that the monument was erected not from spoils but from the ransom" which was paid for the captive prisoners.[31]

---

[30] These may well not be true epitaphs and may, too, represent a new style of monument; but they borrow the traditional epitaphic structure. Cf. Page 219-223.

[31] Raubitschek, no. 168, p. 193; Hdt. 5.77. One wonders if perhaps the transposition of the first and third lines in the later recopying of this epigram (Raubitschek,

Hence, both main clauses (verses 1 and 4) relate to the monument, and purely explanatory material is subordinated.

The distich in Hephaistion, if taken alone as an epigram, violates the major consideration that informs the structure of these other epigrams. There is no explicit mention of the monument; and if the names of the tyrannicides are taken as such a reference, their clause is subordinated to the initial one. Even if these lines were followed by another couplet ending in πατρίδα γῆν ἐθέτην, the resulting lacuna apparently could not satisfy the requirement. We can allow for a certain novelty in a tyrannicide epigram by a famous poet, but it should not violate so firm a structural rule of the epigrams of its day.

While these two objections do not constitute proof, they do lead me to suggest that the lines quoted by Hephaistion could not have stood on any tyrannicide monument, at least not on one erected at any time before Thucydides.[32] Such a conclusion would have to remain tentative and highly conjectural, were it not for the existence of another piece of evidence that might allow us to suggest a new and very different text for an early epigram in honor of Harmodios and Aristogeiton. It might even permit us to postulate a new method for restoring the Agora fragment.

The evidence derives from a small, upright, inscribed stele found in 1956 on Chios.[33] The inscription is dated by its lettering to the

---

no. 173) indicates that people forgot how the original monument had been financed; thus, the epigram seemed to violate a requirement of form. A fragment of the later text, with a commentary, appears at *P. Oxy.* 31.2535. This *hypomnema* may derive from Polemon of Ilium. I owe this reference to Mr. Dirk Obbink.

[32] This conclusion is, of course, not altered by Friedländer's theory, p. 92, that the first distich belonged to the Antenor group, whereas the second was added below it on the new base in 477. I do not know what is behind the statement of H. Berve, *Die Tyrannis bei den Griechen* (Munich 1967) II 562, that on the Agora fragment one finds, "Reste eines zweiten, wohl auf derselben Basis angebrachten Epigramms."

[33] Inv. B.M. 677 in the new Archaeological Museum in Chios town, currently mounted in front of a pillar in the museum's inner courtyard. The *editio princeps*, which I have not seen, is in an article by A. Stephanou in the newspaper Χιακὸς Λαός, December 31, 1956. Stephanou subsequently published the stone in Χιακὰ Μελετήματα 1 (1958) 20 ff. I wish to thank the director of the library in Chios town for securing a copy of this article for me. Other editions and commentaries include: Robert; Trypanis; Podlecki 1973, 32-34, no. 4a; *SEG* 16.497, 17.392. Professor Raubitschek first called my attention to this collection and suggested that it needed to be considered by those investigating the tyrannicide monuments.

The stone is 0.49m high and 0.233 wide, showing original surface on the front, left, rear and top. It is 0.19 thick at the thickest point (about center); but, 0.084

"turn of the third to the second century B.C."[34] The stone's front surface shows what appears to be a collection of seven, two- and four-line poems, each set off from the one below by a *paragraphos* and a blank space. In its reuse as a building block the stone was cut vertically down the middle, so only the left one third to one half of each line survives. Moreover, as the stone is broken off along its bottom edge, there may originally have been more than seven poems. I agree with Trypanis, at least until I have had an opportunity to study the other poems more thoroughly, that each one should be considered a discrete and complete unit rather than part of a longer composition or fragment.[35] Furthermore, with one likely exception, all the poems exhibit the formal characteristics of classical metrical inscriptions. There is no agreement on the function of the stone; Trypanis, in the most extensive treatment to date, suggests that the stele "served, together with other similar stelae, as a text-book in some expensive private school in Chios."[36] No secure evidence has been brought forward for determining whether the epigrams are novel fabrications, imitations of genuine models, or copies of authentic inscriptions. Although the following discussion may throw some light on this problem, more study is needed.

from the left surface, the rear face begins to taper sharply down to a thickness of 0.145 and then tapers more gradually to a thickness of 0.136 at the left edge. Thus, a long vertical tenon is formed on the rear of the stone; apparently the stone was anchored to a wall or other structure with this tenon. The right half of the top surface is broken away, but the left side preserves a roughly square cutting, about 0.05 to a side and 0.02 deep. Presumably the stone bore some sort of finial, or perhaps another stone, which fit into this cutting. If we accept in essence the restorations suggested below, original width would have been ca. 0.460.

[34] Trypanis 70.

[35] This does not rule out the possibility of some overall thematic unity among the poems or a unifying feature common to all, which, if known, would explain the reason for the collection. Robert, while criticizing Stephanou's theory that the poems were all composed specifically for this monument, does raise the possibility that the epigrams were collected from individual monuments in honor of local Chians. I hope to publish an analysis of the entire collection in the near future. Both D.M. Lewis and M.B. Wallace have privately expressed grave doubts about the hypotheses suggested below, mainly because none of the other poems on the stone seems to them to be more than Hellenistic exercises.

[36] Trypanis 74 mentions other collections of epigrams for schools and certain prose inscriptions from Chios that may have been made for academic purposes. Cf. now P.S. Derow and W.G. Forrest, "An Inscription from Chios," *BSA* 77 (1982) 125-176.

It is the fourth poem on the Chian stone that is important for a consideration of the tyrannicides. The text is undisputed:

> στησαιτουτοεδοκη[
> γειτονοσαιχμητ[
> οικτανονανδρατυρα[
> ψυχασπαρθεμενο[

Readings and suggested restorations appear below:

> στῆσαι τοῦτο ἐδόκη[σεν Ἀθηναίοισιν Ἀριστο-]
> γείτονος αἰχμητ[οῦ μνῆμα καὶ Ἁρμοδίου,]
> οἳ κτάνον ἄνδρα τύρα[ννον (˘)- ˘˘ - ˘˘ - ˘]
> ψυχὰς παρθέμενο[ι - ˘ ˘ - ˘ ˘ -].

1,2 suppl. Raubitschek privatim; idem Lloyd-Jones apud Trypanis sed σῆμα pro μνῆμα et fort. αἰχμητ[ῶν; αἰχμητ[αῖς Robert. — 3 τύρα[ννον ἐλεύθερον εὔνομον ἦδε suppl. Raubitschek privatim; τύρα[ννον ἐλευθερίαν τε ˘ - ˘ Maas apud Trypanis. — 4 παρθέμενο[ι πατρίδα γῆν ἐθέτην suppl. Raubitschek privatim; παρθέμενο[ι πατρίδα γῆν ἔθεσαν Maas apud Trypanis.

The restorations of the last two lines are quite uncertain, but those of the first two are secure enough to warrant our accepting the poem as an epigram in honor of the Athenian tyrannicides.[37] The origin of the poem can never be known with certainty, unless further evidence surfaces; but we can perhaps advance the scholarship on the tyrannicides by assuming that the epigram is not a late fabrication, but rather that it derives from the earlier stages of the tradition about Harmodios and Aristogeiton.[38] If this assumption is accepted, and

---

[37] Only Robert raises the possibility that the poem is not about Harmodios and Aristogeiton but about local Chian tyrannicides. I find such an hypothesis implausible in the light of -γείτονος- in the second line; this, together with the act of tyrannicide in the third, surely guarantees the restoration [Ἀριστο-]|γείτονος. This, in turn, demands a mention of Harmodios and it also establishes a certain similarity between this poem and the one in Hephaistion.

[38] Trypanis 71f. refuses to connect the poem from Chios with any of the known monuments and is "inclined to see no. IV as one more anonymous Hellenistic fictitious epigram for the tomb of Harmodios and Aristogeiton"; cf. Berve (above, note 32) 563. For Robert, cf. note 37 above. Podlecki 1973, 32-34, partially anticipated my conclusion by suggesting that the poem may derive from the Antenor base; he rejects both the Kritios base (because of the lines in Hephaistion) and what he calls the only other possible monumental source, namely, the tomb. Taylor 30f., n. 20, is noncommittal.

nothing is found to contradict it, we can conclude that this is a copy, or at least an imitation,[39] of an epigram that stood originally on either the Antenor base only, the Kritios base only, both bases, the tomb in the *demosion sema*, or some otherwise unknown monument. Again, certainty is impossible, but I should like to explore the possibility that this poem (or its model) was composed originally for one of the groups in the Agora. Without further evidence, the discussion will have to be limited to a demonstration of the poem's appropriateness for its suggested role.

In the context of this paper, perhaps the first thing to be noted is that the extant remains and obvious restorations of the Chian epigram avoid the historical and typological problems encountered in the lines in Hephaistion. The first problem stemmed from the manner in which that poem gave greater priority to the liberation of Athens in 510 as the direct political result of the tyrannicides' deed than to that deed itself. The extant portions of the Chian poem avoid that anachronism by concentrating on the monument, the murder, and the heroes' glorious death. This is not to say that the poem is apolitical. The first distich records a political (in the sense of δημοσίᾳ) event; the third line mentions the political position of the victim; and the endings of the last two lines may well have contained a reference to an altered status in the political life of the Athenian state. Still, it can be argued that none of these facts would have forced a reader to associate the assassination with the liberation in the way Hephaistion's poem does. First, references to the erection of the monument and to the erector were normal in epigrams. If the erector named is "the Athenians," so be it. This may tell us something about Athenian constitutional procedures at the time, but it does not reflect a specific version of events leading up to the establishment of that constitution. Second, the description of Hipparchos as ἀνὴρ τύραννος can be interpreted in two senses. While it could refer to his political status among all citizens,[40] we must also remember that "tyrant" did not denote a specific political office and in fact was used to refer to the tyrant's special status

---

[39] In discussion after the oral version of this paper, this possibility was endorsed by Prof. M.B. Walbank, who, together with Prof. D.M. Lewis, rejected my suggestion that the Chian poem is a copy.

[40] Hipparchos' position as (co-)tyrant is explicit in the first, third, and fourth Harmodios skolia and the account of the *Ath. Pol.*; it is implicit in Herodotus. Cf. Fornara 1970, 165f.

vis-à-vis the other nobles, a status that smacked of hybris.[41] If the skolia are any guide, this latter sense seems to have been primary in the earlier tradition about Harmodios and Aristogeiton. Finally, any reference to Athens' altered political situation in the lacunae of the second distich would clearly be subordinated to the heroes' monument, deed, and death. Moreover, it may well have had more to do with what we might call the moral meaning of the deed itself— a noble blow that showed that tyrant-types were no longer above ancestral custom and its just retribution — than with such political consequences of the deed as either the liberation of 510 or the institution of democracy.[42] Hence, nothing in the poem would necessarily have forced a reader to interpret the statuary group as a monument to the liberation rather than, what it literally was, a memorial depicting two heroic men who died in the act of murder.

My second objection to the lines quoted by Hephaistion was that they do not contain a reference to the monument on which they are supposed to have stood, nor do they adequately reflect one of the traditional types of epigram. The Chian poem, by contrast, begins with a reference to the monument (τοῦτο), which seems to have been followed by a rather good description of the sculptural groups as we know them: [μνῆμα ’Αριστο]γείτονος [καὶ ’Αρμοδίου,] οἳ κτάνον... ψυχὰς παρθέμενο[ι. The monument itself is primary; the reason for its erection is contained in the relative clause. Concerning the matter of typology, the Chian epigram is almost overly interested in defining the monument for which it was originally composed. In fact, one can point to internal evidence for identifying the monument as a public decree, or an epitaph, or even a dedication. Taylor calls the poem a "versified decree," in reference no doubt to εδοκη[with its reasonable supplement as ἐδόκη[σεν ’Αθηναίοισιν.[43] In favor of an epitaph, one can

----

[41] The tyrant usurps the "freedom" of the other nobles to compete on equal grounds for honor. This freedom was expressed in the late archaic period by the term ἰσονομία, the adjectival form of which figures prominently in the first and last Harmodios skolia. Cf. Fornara 1970, 174-178.

[42] Cf. Fornara *ibid.*

[43] Taylor 30, n. 20. While ἔδοξεν would be normal in an Attic decree of the period, ἐδόκησεν is supported by uses in tragedy and presumably by metrical considerations. It should also be noted that forms of ἵστημι can be used in decrees for the setting up of the stele bearing the decree; cf. *IG* I², 56 = I³, 156, lines 24, 29; I², 70, line 21 (but cf. I³, 73, line 7); see also I², 371, line 17 = I³, 472, line 154. For an interesting, if later, parallel, cf. Hansen no. 431; a decree, presumably recording the

point to: (1) the emphasis on the manner of the heroes' death in the phrase ψυχὰς παρθέμενο[ι;[44] (2) the poem's structure, with the monument referred to by a demonstrative, the name of the deceased in the genitive, and an amplification of the dead person's accomplishments in a relative clause;[45] (3) the possibility that τοῦτο modified σῆμα;[46] (4) the use of forms of ἵστημι on funerary monuments.[47] Still, of the foregoing characteristics, only the word σῆμα would not be appropriate for a dedication as well as an epitaph. The transitive use of ἵστημι, for example, is common in Ionic dedications of statues and also appears in Attic examples.[48]

An epigram of such mixed nature might be appropriate for the statues of the tyrannicides in the Agora, which themselves seem to have served more than one purpose. They depicted men who had died in the pursuance of a noble, but violent, deed; hence, an epigram reminiscent of a soldier's epitaph would not have been out of place. Moreover, an epitaph might be expected on a monument that served as the focal point of a hero-cult, and there is no proof that the hero-cult of the tyrannicides belonged to the *demosion sema* rather than the Agora.[49] Also as heroes, of course, Harmodios and Aristogeiton would

circumstances of the erection of the monument, accompanies an epigram on the stone. The decree begins with the formulaic, [ἔδοξ]εν τ[ῆι βο(υ)λῆι, κτλ.

[44] For this term, see below, page 41.

[45] For parallels, cf. Hansen nos. 27, 39, 42, 46, 51 (unless ὥστε for ὅς τε), 58.

[46] σῆμα would certify this as an epitaph, whereas μνῆμα could appear in a dedication or an epitaph.

[47] Cf. Hansen, with σῆμα, nos. 14, 16, 74, 165; with μνῆμα, nos. 96, 119, 122, 161; also nos. 78, 108, 109, 117, 121, 164.

[48] For Ionic examples, cf. M.L. Lazzarini, *Le formule delle dediche votive nella Grecia arcaica* (Rome 1976) 72; Hansen nos. 316, 390, 410, 414, 424, 429. In Hansen no. 99, which is an epitaph, the word is used in a dependent clause and its object is not the grave marker but τρόπαια; the same usage appears at Hansen no. 177, line 11; Timoth. 791. 196 (ed. Page, above, note 10); Soph. *Trach.* 1102; Ar. *Plut.* 453; Xen. *Hell.* 2.4.7; Isoc. *Paneg.* 87,150; *IG* II², 1457, line 26. The form στῆσε appears in the normal Attic dedication, Hansen no. 194, and possibly also in 246. Cf. Hansen nos. 313, 317, 322, 325, 339, 415, 442. Cf. also the epigrams in the literary tradition, Page 194f. Forms of ἵστημι also appear in many of the testimonia for the tyrannicide groups; cf. Brunnsåker (above, note 7) 33ff., nos. 1-3, 4a, 5-11.

[49] For the connection of the cult with an early Antenor group, cf. Taylor 20; for the location of the annual sacrifice to Harmodios and Aristogeiton, *ibid.* 22f., where the grave of the tyrannicides is mentioned. If the sacrifice was not held in the Agora, still, the heroic nature of the statues would have been obvious, and the tyrannicides themselves were certainly "the subjects of a popular reverence, religious in nature"

have been worthy of dedications; and to some extent we should consider the statuary groups to be dedications to them, after the fashion, say, of an Athena Promachos striding forward toward imagined enemies.[50] However, instead of a traditional formula of dedication to such new heroes—perhaps too unconventional—, the composer chose στῆσαι τοῦτο ἐδοκ[κτλ. This is difficult, partly because it seems unpoetic and partly because it is without exact parallel; but it may not be impossible. The groups were set up at public expense in a location that was kept free of other statues of people.[51] Antenor's group may even have been the first great public monument of the democracy. It would thus seem appropriate to record on the monument the decree mandating its erection. One would expect such a decree to be in prose and separate from the epigram,[52] but Podlecki points to a possible parallel from the literary tradition for, in essence, bringing the decree (δημοσίᾳ in this case) into the epigram:[53]

> Δίρφυος ἐδμήθημεν ὑπὸ πτυχί, σῆμα δ' ἐφ' ἡμῖν
> ἐγγύθεν Εὐρίπου δημοσίᾳ κέχυται·...

In any case, the composer of an epigram for a new type of monument may either invent a new kind of epigram or adapt traditional types to suit the new requirements. If the Chian poem belongs to either Agora group, its author clearly chose the second alternative; he created a combination of epitaph, dedication, and public decree.

What has been seen so far of the Chian epigram suggests some degree of authenticity; it seems unlikely that a Hellenistic poetaster could have gotten so much right without a genuine model. Still, can we say this is a copy rather than an imitation? Again, proof must

---

(Taylor 21). Cf. now, C.W. Clairmont, *Patrios Nomos* ("BAR International Series," 161 [i]; Oxford 1983), I 2f., 14, 22f., 220f.

[50] Or after the fashion of kouroi, if the epigram was on Antenor's base and that group was a pair of late-archaic kouroi; cf. note 26 above.

[51] That these were the only statues of people in the Agora before the end of the fifth century, cf. Demosth. 20.70. For a hesitancy to set up dedications in public places (esp. in the Agora) to honor living people, cf. the issue of the Kimonian herms at Aeschin. 3.183f.

[52] Cf. Hansen no. 431.

[53] Podlecki 1973, 33; Page 191. Podlecki admires the "simplicity of the wording" in the Chian poem; Lewis could not, however, accept it as genuinely early, and Wallace has reminded me how convincingly Hellenistic imitators could word an epigram.

remain elusive, but some contribution might be made by considering the poem's diction and structure. If everything is acceptable for a date between 510 and 477, we shall perhaps have gone as far as we can go.

First, the diction. The quasi-formulaic usage of the first line and the meaning of τύρα[ννον have been discussed above. For the splitting of Aristogeiton's name one need only refer to the literature on the lines in Hephaistion. There remain:

1. αἰχμητής, although not literally true of the tyrannicides, is well-attested in Homer and other early poetry as a generic term meaning "warlike," "warrior," or simply "brave." It can be seen as a typically epigrammatic flourish that adds stature to the tyrannicides through association with the language of Homer. More specifically, it associates their deed with military heroism.[54]

2. Although the first aorist of κτείνω and forms of ἀποκτείνω predominate in later references to the tyrannicides, both the first and second aorist of κτείνω are regular in archaic poetry. More to the point, the parallelism among οἵ κτάνον ἄνδρα τύρα[ννον here, ὅτε/ὅτι τὸν τύραννον κτανέτην in the first and fourth of the Harmodios skolia, and ὅτε... ἄνδρα τύραννον Ἵππαρχον ἐκαινέτην in the third skolion can hardly be accidental. One cannot prove that the Chian epigram is not a late imitation of the skolia, but it is equally possible that both skolia and epigram derive from a common tradition which was expressed in a conventional, probably rhythmical or even metrical, phrasing.

3. The expression ψυχὰς παρθέμενοι, apparently meaning something like "hazarding their lives," occurs in the same metrical position in Homer, and similar expressions occur elsewhere in Homer and in Tyrtaios.[55] The latter applies the expression to the man who stands

---

[54] One might even go a bit further: Could the (*sc.* ἀνὴρ) αἰχμητής be consciously contrasted with the ἀνὴρ τύραννος? For ἄνδρες αἰχμηταί, cf. Hom. *Il.* 3.49, 17.740; for the singular, cf. the epigram Hansen no. 19. For αἰχμητής as an epithet of θυμός, cf. Pin. *Nem.* 9.37. In the following Homeric passages, some form of αἰχμητής appears in the same metrical position as in our pentameter; in examples marked with an asterisk, the word follows a personal name with which it agrees: *Il.* 1.290; *5.706; 6.97 = 278; 7.281; *11.739; 12.419; *13.171; 17.588; *Od.* *2.19; 16.242.

[55] The expression occurs three times within the same formulaic address to strangers, where it is applied to pirates: *Od.* 3.74; 9.255; *Hym. Ap.* 455. At *Od.* 2.237, σφὰς γὰρ παρθέμενοι is applied to the suitors; cf. W.B. Stanford (ed.), *The Odyssey of Homer* (London 1964) I 242, who comments: "the metaphor is from gambling, 'staking their heads.'" Tyrtaios, 12.18, made the term more respectable in the line, ψυχὴν καὶ θυμὸν

ἐν προμάχοισι and thus is ἐσθλός and ἀγαθός for his πόλις and δῆμος. The sentiment is appropriate for the tyrannicides, who were to be associated closely with the Athenian dead of the Persian War.[56]

If the suggested restorations of the Chian poem's first two and a half lines are essentially correct, their structure is admirably simple and traditional. One can also suggest perfectly acceptable restorations for the last line, *e.g.*:[57]

> ψυχὰς παρθέμενο[ι καὶ πατρίδ᾽ εὐκλέϊσαν].

It seems to be generally assumed, however, that the lacuna in the third line must complete a verbal expression at the end of the fourth, in which case ψυχὰς παρθέμενο[ι would seem to break up the sense intolerably.[58] In the first place, this assumption need not be made; one could, *e.g.*, restore the second distich as follows:[59]

> οἳ κτάνον ἄνδρα τύρα[ννον ὅτ᾽ ἐν θυσίαισιν ᾽Αθηνᾶς]
> ψυχὰς παρθέμενο[ι εὐκλέϊσαν πατρίδα].

Moreover, even if ψυχὰς παρθέμενο[ι does interrupt a unit, the structure should not be considered fatally flawed. Hansen no. 2 seems to show a similar interruption:

> ...ἔσχον γὰρ πεζοί τε [καὶ] ⌊ὀκυπόρον ἐπὶ νεδ⌋ν ⫶
> ℎελλά[δα μ]ὲ πᾶσαν δούλιο⌊ν ἔμαρ ἰδὲν⌋.

If one accepts the historical content, typology, diction, and structure of the Chian epigram as appropriate for one of the Agora monuments, one must then ask whether the poem is more likely to have stood on one monument than on the other. The grounds for

---

τλήμονα παρθέμενος. For a similar expression in a later (?432 B.C.) epigram which is reminiscent of the Tyrtaios passage, cf. Hansen no. 10, lines 9-12. The negative statement of the same sentiment may be found at Solon 13.46: φειδωλὴν ψυχῆς οὐδεμίαν θέμενος...

[56] The evidence is gathered by Taylor 23f.

[57] Cf. Hansen nos. 6 and 10.

[58] According to Lewis, this is a major stumbling block for any who would accept the poem as authentic. He admits, however, that such thinking may well be influenced by the attempt to restore the last line from the Agora fragment, πα]τρίδα γῆν, which would demand a complement in the third line.

[59] The third skolion reads, ὅτ᾽ ᾽Αθηναίης ἐν θυσίαις. For εὐκλέϊσαν πατρίδα, cf. Hansen no. 6. The form ᾽Αθηνᾶς, of course, poses a serious problem, for which cf. L. Threatte, *The Grammar of Attic Inscriptions* I (Berlin and New York 1980) 271f.

answer are totally subjective, but the simplicity of the first distich suggested to Podlecki at least the earlier group, that by Antenor.[60] This, if true, would raise a further question: Could an early Athenian epigram, unknown in the extant literary tradition, have found its way to Hellenistic Chios? Negative arguments might seem to be telling, but they are necessarily *e silentio*; positive ones, while difficult, may not be impossible. For example, the old Antenor base may have been preserved after the loss of the statues.[61] This problem would, of course, disappear if the epigram stood on the Kritios-Nesiotes base; any traveler between Athens and Chios might have known the text.[62] However, this possibility seems to be ruled out by the association of the later base with the Agora fragment. Thus, one last question arises. Could the Chian poem be a copy of "the epigram of which a fragment was found in the Agora?"[63]

The resulting restoration would read:

στῆσαι τοῦτο ἐδόκη[σεν Ἀθηναίοισιν Ἀριστο-]
γείτονος αἰχμητ[οῦ μνῆμα καὶ] ⌊Ἁρμοδίου,⌋
οἳ κτάνον ἄνδρα τύρα[ννον (⌣)- ⌣̆⌣ - ⌣ ⌣ - ⌣]
ψυχὰς παρθέμενο[ι πα]⌊τρίδα γῆν ἐθέτην⌋.

Two problems must be dealt with in justifying this text. The first is the less serious, namely, the switch from plural to dual in the last line. The Chian copyist might simply have changed unfamiliar duals to plurals; there is no significant difference between the scansion of παρθεμένω... ἐθέτην and of παρθέμενοι... ἔθεσαν. The easiest solution, however, is to accept the switch in number; a plural participle may be used with a dual verb.[64] The harder problem is the restoration of the third line.

If πατρίδα γῆν ἐθέτην were able to stand on its own,[65] the restoration might be simple. However, πατρίδα γῆν is a set phrase that

[60] Podlecki 1973, 33.

[61] Cf. Trypanis 72; Podlecki *ibid.* Other possibilities may well exist. A study of the whole Chian collection might shed some light on this problem.

[62] Taylor 189, n. 6, gathers the evidence for the popularity of the tyrannicides outside of Athens.

[63] Raubitschek, *per epistulam.*

[64] H.W. Smyth, *Greek Grammar²* (Cambridge, Mass. 1956), sect. 1045; R. Kühner, *Ausführliche Grammatik der griechischen Sprache* II, 1 (Hannover and Leipzig 1898) 71f., where attention is called to *Il.* 4.452f., and Pin. *Ol.* 2.87.

[65] A casual suggestion made privately by Prof. M. Chambers. The literal translation would thus be, presumably, "...made their land a fatherland."

demands a complement at the end of the third line.[66] Both suggested restorations of the line have problems. Maas' ἐλευθερίαν τε ‿ - ⌣ is difficult to complete sensibly, and Raubitschek's ἐλεύθερον εὔνομον ἤδε presents us with a rather severe asyndeton. Moreover, especially if the epigram is older than the Persian War, we should expect forms of ἰσονομία rather than ἐλευθερία. I cannot suggest a restoration in which one could place much confidence; however, one might read, *e.g.*:

οἳ κτάνον ἄνδρα τύρα[ννον ὅτ᾿ εὔνομον ἐν θυσίαισιν].

In any case, since a restoration that is satisfactorily simple and direct seems to be possible, we cannot rule out the hypothesis that the Chian poem and the Agora fragment belong together.

One could certainly wish that our evidence were more concrete and that the poem from Chios had been engraved in better company; yet that poem seems to contain some authentic recollection of the early tradition about the tyrannicides and it is appropriate for the Agora monuments. As in the case of so many poems in the *Anthology*, one cannot prove that the Chian piece is not a skillful Hellenistic fiction. But on other hand, there seems to be as much reason for connecting it with the original tyrannicide monuments as for associating them with the lines in Hephaistion.[67]

In conclusion, let us return to the topic from which we launched into this analysis of epigrams, namely, the popular tradition about the murder of Hipparchos. We classicists cannot imitate our colleagues in modern social history; we cannot tape-record interviews with large numbers of ancient Athenians. However, to some extent we can identify what beliefs those people generally held about their city's past, even the very recent past, and what were the nature and intensity of their emotional reactions to those beliefs. This is a tricky business, but I think the Athenian tyrannicides provide us with a case in point.

The tyrannicide groups in the Agora were extremely important to the people of Athens. Their location itself was significant, and no other statues of people were allowed in the vicinity until the Hellenistic period. We know next to nothing about the Antenor group, unless

---

[66] For πατρίδα γῆν, see Hansen nos. 80, 82, 101, 143; cf. no. 66.

[67] Soon after the discovery of the Agora fragment, some scholars were cautious about identifying it with the lines in Hephaistion; cf. D.M. Robinson, *CP* 33 (1938) 211, n. 6; C. Picard, *REG* 50 (1937) 118.

it was the prototype of the later one; but that replacement group was immensely popular. It was imitated and copied for centuries, and Aristophanes could even make a joke about the statues' pose and expect his audience to get it.[68] I suspect that we can make some fairly safe assumptions about the emotional reactions of average, patriotic Athenians as they stopped and gazed at the monument. The statues themselves would have inspired a powerful awe before their imposing physical presence and violent action. Furthermore, their "stop action" poses would call to mind the whole narrative of the assassination, which occupied an important place in the folklore of every native Athenian. Knowledge of the narrative, then, would carry the emotional reaction created by the artwork over to the viewers' evaluation of the event depicted—I mean a sense of almost religious wonder at the glorious deed and heroic deaths of Harmodios and Aristogeiton, a desire to emulate them, and a feeling of pride in the city that produced such fine citizens and such fine statues.

Finally, of course, our hypothetical viewers would approach and read the epigram. We should not doubt that Athenians regularly stopped and read such epigrams. Even humble funerary and votive monuments of this period bore epigrams that were meant to be read. On the whole, these small literary compositions did not say surprising things; they confirmed the emotional reaction created by the artwork and they limited their remarks to the conventional. This is why monuments with epigrams that commemorate important historical events are so important to the student of popular traditions. It is virtually axiomatic that, in Greek art and poetry, conventional approaches to historical events were a necessary condition for the enthusiastic response of hearers and viewers.

The poem on the stone in Chios would meet these requirements quite well if it were inscribed on the base of the statues of Harmodios and Aristogeiton. It confirms the emotions that the statues would have stirred, namely, awe, emulation, and civic pride; and it reproduces faithfully the popular conception of the tyrannicides; that is, it honors the heroes and their deed without necessarily associating that deed with either the liberation from tyranny or the institution of the democracy. This agrees nicely with Fornara's contention that Thucydides did not castigate the popular tradition for associating the murder with the liberation, but for overestimating the significance

[68] *Lys.* 630 ff.

of the murder itself. And the deed was overestimated precisely because of the emotional power it commanded in the hearts of most Athenians.

Fornara, C.W., 1968. "The 'Tradition' about the Murder of Hipparchus," *Historia* 17, 400-424.

Fornara, C.W., 1970. "The Cult of Harmodius and Aristogeiton," *Philologus* 114, 155-180.

Friedländer, P., 1938. "Geschichtswende im Gedicht," *StItal* N.S. 15, 89-93.

Hansen, P.A., 1983. *Carmina Epigraphica Graeca* (Berlin and New York).

Meritt, B.D., 1936. "Greek Inscriptions," *Hesperia* 5, 355-358, no. 1.

Page, D.L., 1981. *Further Greek Epigrams* (Cambridge). All references are to pages.

Podlecki, A.J., 1966. "The Political Significance of the Athenian 'Tyrannicide'-Cult," *Historia* 15, 129-141.

Podlecki, A.J., 1973. *"Epigraphica Simonidea," Epigraphica* 35, 24-39.

Raubitschek, A.E., 1949. *Dedications from the Athenian Akropolis* (Cambridge, Mass.).

Robert, J. and L., *REG* 71 (1958) 294f., no. 379 = *BEpigr* 1958, 379.

Taylor, M.W., *The Tyrant Slayers* (New York 1981 = Diss. Harvard 1975).

Trypanis, C.A., 1960. "A New Collection of Epigrams from Chios," *Hermes* 88, 69-74.

Practical Knowledge and the Historian's Role in Herodotus and Thucydides

CAROLYN DEWALD
University of Southern California

In one sense, history writing for the Greeks began with Homer. In another more formal sense, history was not only a new literary genre but a radically new kind of genre when Herodotus and Thucydides began to write in the fifth century B.C. Because Herodotus and Thucydides wrote in prose, what they wrote was open ended in a way that poetry had never been. The first historians had to make explicit in their texts both the nature of their subject matter and the authorial stances that they intended to take.[1]

We owe the genre of history to the fact that Herodotus and Thucydides define their tasks as authors in similar ways. Both of them make it clear that they have decided to narrate what happened in the recent human past — a past, that is, still accessible to living memory

[1] For Homer and the literary antecedents of history writing, see H. Strasburger, *Homer und die Geschichtsschreibung* (Heidelberg 1972) and *Die Wesensbestimmung der Geschichte durch die antike Geschichtsschreibung* (Wiesbaden 1966). For the beginning of history writing among the Greeks, see R. Drews, *The Greek Accounts of Eastern History* (Washington, D.C. 1973) and A. Momigliano, "Greek Historiography," *History and Theory* 17 (1978) 1-28, esp. Appendix I. The most recent assessment of the problem is that of C. Fornara, *The Nature of History in Ancient Greece and Rome* (Berkeley 1983).

and from which some evidence exists against which to test the witness of memory. From this past, they both choose to narrate an event monumental in scope; the focus of the narrative alternates between large-scale social movements and the role of specific individuals within these movements.[2] Discussing their own role as authors, both state that they are interested in accuracy about the facts they narrate. Both insist on the fact that accuracy is difficult to achieve, and they describe some of the techniques they have developed to guard against error.[3]

One equally important part of their method remains implicit. As readers, we feel that Herodotus and Thucydides have not just narrated but have explained events, in part because of the consistency of the patterns of human behavior they depict.[4] Here I want to focus on one aspect of these patterns: how Herodotus and Thucydides represent informed and effective political behavior. I will examine the kind of practical knowledge that enables people in their histories to make

[2] For the change in the concept of time, see M. von Leyden, "Spatium Historicum," *Durham University Journal* 11 (1949-1950) 89-104; F. Châtelet, "Le temps de l'histoire et l'évolution de la fonction historienne," *Journal de psychologie* 53 (1956); P. Vidal-Naquet, "Temps des dieux et temps des hommes," in *Le chasseur noir. Formes de pensée et formes de société dans le monde grec* (Paris 1981) 69-94. See also the broader implications discussed by A. Momigliano in "Tradition and the Classical Historian," *Essays in Ancient and Modern Historiography* (Middletown, Connecticut 1977) 161-177, and by M. Finley in "Myth, Memory and History," *The Use and Abuse of History* (New York 1971) 11-33.

[3] Thucydides briefly discusses his own authorial procedures in 1.20-22 and 5.26. Herodotus makes no explicit statement on method, but scattered throughout his history are brief critical comments assessing the quality of his evidence (e.g.: 1.182; 4.105; 5.54; 6.53; 6.124). For a recent assessment of Thucydides' method, see P. Pouncey, *The Necessities of War: A Study of Thucydides' Pessimism* (New York 1980) 9-29. The most systematic investigation of Herodotus' method remains that of H. Verdin, *De historisch-kritische Methode van Herodotus* (Brussels 1971). See also ch.4 of my forthcoming study, *The Voice of the* Histōr: *Narrator and Narrative in Herodotus' History*.

[4] Thucydides clearly points to this aspect of historical narrative in 1.22: ὅσοι δὲ βουλήσονται τῶν τε γενομένων τὸ σαφὲς σκοπεῖν καὶ τῶν μελλόντων ποτὲ αὖθις κατὰ τὸ ἀνθρώπινον τοιούτων καὶ παραπλησίων ἔσεσθαι, ὠφέλιμα κρίνειν αὐτὰ ἀρκούντως ἕξει. What he meant is still very much under debate. See A. Gomme, *A Historical Commentary on Thucydides* 1 (Oxford 1950) 149-150. The problem of the usefulness of history is closely related to the contemporary debate about history's status as a social science. For an intelligent survey of the issues, see most recently R. Atkinson, *Knowledge and Explanation in History* (Ithaca 1978). V. Hunter offers an interesting but problematic comparison of narrative patterns in Herodotus and Thucydides: *Past and Process in Herodotus and Thucydides* (Princeton 1982).

effective political decisions. I will argue that the two historians define effective practical knowledge and its relation to political action quite differently, but that each adopts a model that remains consistent throughout his own text. This model does not just underlie the actions of the individual actors within the narrative; it also shows us important aspects of how Herodotus and Thucydides perceived their tasks as authors. The two historians work in quite different ways, with different standards of what constitutes good history. Each, however, adopts authorial attitudes and procedures that resemble the behavior of the most successful actors they depict. I will conclude by suggesting what this shows about the intellectual generation of which Herodotus was an older and Thucydides a younger member.

These questions are large ones and it would be impossible to treat them here with the degree of completeness that they deserve. I advance in this learned company only one justification for the ambitious scope of this paper. It was Professor Raubitschek who taught me, as a beginning scholar and teacher, to look always to the largest questions, since it is in the context of the whole that the individual issues find their meanings. This essay is written from *l'esprit de l'escalier*, as the continuation of an ongoing dialogue that Professor Raubitschek once initiated, about Thucydides and Herodotus as members of the Greek enlightenment. I doubt very much that he will agree with everything said here; I hope, however, that he will accept it as a tribute to his own understanding of Herodotus and Thucydides and to his large capacity to set others asking difficult questions they had not asked before.

To begin, then, with the connections that Herodotus and Thucydides establish in their narratives between human knowledge and action. Eastern kings in Herodotus often receive signs of impending disaster from the gods. Croesus, Astyages, and Xerxes misinterpret the oracles, dreams, and portents that predict the end of their power. If we look at the narrative of events, however, what actually brings these and other rulers to defeat is a very practical kind of ignorance. Croesus dismisses his army too soon after an indecisive battle. He underestimates the boldness of his opponent, Cyrus, and does not anticipate the tactical use Cyrus will make of camels to render his own cavalry ineffective (1.77.4; 1.80.5). Astyages puts in charge of his army a man whose son he has cannibalized (1.127.2). Darius undertakes an invasion of Scythia without understanding the nature of the men and country against whom he marches; he realizes belatedly that in entrusting the bridge to the Ionians, he has risked his kingdom and his army. Only the Ionians' own self-interested docility preserves him from disaster (4.133; 4.137; 7.10*a*; 7.10*γ*). In his Greek campaign, Xerxes prefers the advice of an ambitious relative over that of his two most experienced Greek advisors. The scene in 8.68-69 exposes the frivolity of Xerxes' political decision making. There Artemisia delivers one of the most intelligent speeches in the *Histories*. She sets out a strategic and tactical course that will give victory to Xerxes if it is followed. Xerxes is pleased with Artemisia's frankness and intelligence but he ignores her advice. He decides that his own presence at the impending battle will inspire his troops with an enthusiasm sufficient to outweigh all her arguments (8.69.2). Herodotus believes that a divine pattern exists and is foreshadowed by the signs and portents.[5] What really counts in the narrative of events, however, is the ignorance of their actual circumstances that eastern kings habitually display. They will not, or cannot, take account of all of the physical and political determinants of their situations, and their plans fail in consequence.

Eastern kings interest Herodotus; it is part of his purpose in writing the *Histories* to contrast the political habits of East and West. But the behavior I have just described is not just an eastern peculiarity. Political leaders of all nationalities misjudge actions they are about to undertake. Polycrates of Samos underestimates a rival's ruthlessness and goes to his death (3.122-125). Apries loses his temper and has the nose and ears of a trusted advisor lopped off, creating the demoralization in his ranks that will ultimately cost him his throne (2.162.5-6). Megacles naively assumes that children will result from a marriage arranged between his daughter and Pisistratus (1.61). The Spartans ultimately agree to march to Plataea, but they do so only at the last minute, when a Tegean points out that it is in their self-interest (9.9). Whether a particular course of action succeeds or not, Herodotus frequently orders the narrative sequence to show political leaders misunderstanding the nature of the events in which they are engaged. When success occurs, it is by chance or by the exercise of trickery, not because an individual has prudently and capably worked for the desired outcome.[6]

[5] See J. Kirchberg, *Die Funktion der Orakel im Werke Herodots* (Göttingen 1965) 116-120, for the parallels between the role of the oracle and that of the historian, working after the event to reconstitute the pattern.

[6] Plutarch's *De Herodoti malignitate* (*Moralia* 854E-874C) contains an impressive collection of examples, though Plutarch misinterprets their significance. See Ph.-E.

The narrative of events often includes a physical object whose silent presence attests aspects of the situation unnoticed by the participants. The most famous of these objects is, of course, the dinner lying on Harpagus' plate as he sups with his royal master (1.119.4). But the *Histories* are full of comparable objects. Tombs are in fact cenotaphs, bowls have false engravings etched upon them, pyramids and statues generate by their very presence lying stories purporting to explain their creation (9.85; 1.51; 2.134; 2.131). Very few individuals, whether actors inside the account or Herodotus' own informants, can interpret such objects correctly. Atossa argues with her royal husband that it will be good for Persian morale if he undertakes a scouting trip to Greece. The scene is set in the royal bedroom, and her bosom is the clue to the reality of the situation that escapes Darius: a Greek physician and royal slave has cured Atossa of a breast abscess and she has been taught, *didachtheisa*, by him to make the arguments she presents as her own (3.133-134). The unfortunate Barcaeans take their oath standing over the hidden trench that is the sign of their Persian opponent's treachery (4.201). Zopyrus' nose is not the sign of mistreatment that he tells the Babylonians it is; if they were able to read it correctly, they would see it as a sign instead of Zopyrus' loyalty to Darius and the depth of his determination to defeat them (3.157).[7]

Herodotus' pessimism about the possibility of informed political understanding bears affinities to a very old Greek belief. Archaic literature is full of the notion that those who trust in their own power are punished by the gods for their arrogance. Herodotus preserves the substance and even perhaps the theological underpinnings of the earlier stories.[8] The narrative structure of the *Histories*, however, gives at least as much emphasis to the secular and rational causal connections that link successive events. The major political actors in the *Histories* come to grief in their plans because they lack a very practical kind of understanding. Sometimes Herodotus believes that such actors ought to have taken the trouble to find out more about the circumstances surrounding them; sometimes he appears to believe them

Legrand, "De la malignité d'Hérodote," in *Mélanges Gustave Glotz* 2 (Paris 1932) 535-547.

[7] No one has to my knowledge explored the suggestive parallels between Herodotus' use of objects and that of Attic drama. For the latter, see O. Taplin, *Greek Tragedy in Action* (Berkeley 1978) 77-100.

[8] For a full development of this theme, see H. Lloyd-Jones, *The Justice of Zeus* (Berkeley 1971) 58-69.

at fault only because they think they are in charge.[9] He is less interested in distinguishing between these two kinds of failure of knowledge than in showing in practical terms how both kinds work in concrete situations to affect the outcome of events.

Two groups of actors in the *Histories* are partially exempted from this pessimistic picture of human inadequacy to understand and control the course of events. Herodotus presents a number of savants as genuine wise men.[10] One aspect of their knowledge is theoretical. One of the first episodes Herodotus recounts is the story of Solon and Croesus. Solon understands the truth that political leaders ignore; he knows the limitations that the gods have placed on men's knowledge and control over their lives (1.30-33). Herodotus does not usually present his savants, however, as abstract moralists. Solon himself has left Athens in pursuit of *theōriē*, to see the variety of phenomena in the world (1.30.1). Other savants possess an abstract understanding that Herodotus shows to be relevant in political decision making, and they try to make this understanding available to those in charge of events. Thales (in a story Herodotus does not believe) helps an army by rerouting a river around it (1.75); either Bias of Priene or Pittacus of Mytilene discourages Croesus from building a fleet by a timely analogy (1.27). The Ionians receive much good advice from individual savants that they ignore. Thales advises the Ionians to subordinate their individual states into a larger whole, and Bias tells them all to move to Sardinia (1.170). Hecataeus tries to discourage the Ionians from revolt, drawing on his considerable knowledge of the Persian empire (5.36). He also advises Aristagoras in defeat, and both times

---

[9] Herodotus suggests that the gods, whoever they are, seem to share his own sense of the usefulness of an alert practical intelligence. In 1.91.4-5, Apollo tells Croesus that in consulting the oracle Croesus did not make a careful enough investigation of the oracular response (οὐ συλλαβὼν δὲ τὸ ῥηθὲν οὐδ' ἐπανειρόμενος). H. Bischoff, "Der Warner bei Herodot," in W. Marg, ed., *Herodot: Eine Auswahl aus der neueren Forschung* (Darmstadt 1962) 310-312, points out that one of the functions of the bystander or advice-giver in Herodotean narrative is to discuss those aspects of the situation that Herodotus thinks were important but not understood adequately by the principal actors in events.

[10] Both the *Warner* of H. Bischoff, *Der Warner bei Herodot* (diss. Marburg 1932), and the wise advisor of R. Lattimore, "The Wise Advisor in Herodotus," *CP* 34 (1939) 24-35, should be seen as aspects of this larger context. Herodotus is not always supportive of the efforts of Greek intellectuals. See Ph.-E. Legrand, *Hérodote. Histoires* 1 (Paris 1966) 146.

his advice is ignored (5.125-126). The Ionians dismiss the practical advice of Dionysius the Phocaean as well (6.12). As Herodotus presents it, ignorance and amateurism play as large a part in the Ionian loss of freedom as they do in Xerxes' later invasion of Greece. In general, Herodotus believes that some informed individuals understand important facts about politics, geography, and military tactics and are willing to apply their information in the sphere of practical politics. Their advice is almost never taken by those in power.

The other group of actors to whom Herodotus allows some understanding of events are at first glance hard to assimilate into this neat division between doers and knowers. Some actors in the *Histories* succeed in their political aims by unconventional or manipulative behavior that makes them resemble the trickster figures of folktale.[11] We have already discussed Artemisia of Halicarnassus as one of Xerxes' most astute advisors. She saves her ship at Salamis by extremely unconventional and even deplorable behavior: she sinks an allied ship, with the result that the Greeks pursuing her think that she must be part of their own fleet and turn their attention elsewhere (8.87). Themistocles lies, manipulates, and bribes his way to Greek victory; at the moment of his greatest military success Herodotus depicts him mouthing pious platitudes with one hand and secretly preparing to feather his Persian nest with the other (8.5; 8.22; 8.75; 8.109-110). Miltiades begins a career in the Chersonese by taking prisoner those gathered to mourn his brother's death (6.39). Maiandrius preserves his power at Samos by abandoning his egalitarian ideals and treacherously jailing his opponents; his brother kills them (3.142-143). Hermotimus the eunuch takes what Herodotus terms the most successful revenge known to him by tricking his enemy into his power with promises of *agatha*. Once his enemy's family lies in Hermotimus' power, he proceeds to castrate them all (8.105-106). Herodotus' apparent zest at retelling unconventional, manipulative, and treacherous achievements has disturbed critics from Plutarch's day until the present. Legrand remarks: "En un mot, l'habileté, même associée à l'indélicatesse, trouve trop facilement grâce devant lui."[12]

---

[11] The most thorough and suggestive consideration of the intelligence of the trickster is that of M. Detienne and J.-P. Vernant, *Les ruses de l'intelligence. La métis des Grecs* (Paris 1974).

[12] See Legrand (above, note 10) 125.

If we look only at their superficial characteristics, the savants and the tricksters in the *Histories* appear to be radically different types. The savants are detached but interested onlookers of the political scene; they do not act themselves but give good advice to others that is generally ignored. The trickster figures, on the other hand, manipulate situations for their own benefit, in order to accomplish their own political ends. When they seek to persuade others to a course of action, they speak deceitfully; unlike the savants, they usually succeed. They persuade others to do what they want, or they do it themselves through deception. Such figures often know how to read the signs of physical objects correctly. Thrasybulus of Miletus lops the tops off the tallest ears of wheat; his fellow tyrant, Periander, reads the sign correctly and proceeds to massacre the most outstanding of his citizens (5.92ζ). Cleomenes of Sparta twice reads the message implicit in a physical object and saves himself from political misjudgment in consequence. He recognizes that Maiandrius' goblet is an implicit attempt to divert his judgment by bribery (3.148). When Aristagoras tries to plead the Ionian cause with the help of a bronze map, Cleomenes forces Aristagoras to reveal the secret contained in the map: Aristagoras is asking him to embark on a journey of three months' distance from home (5.49-50).

Some trickster figures even create the objects that mislead others. Thrasybulus sets out lavish banquets to suggest Miletus' ease and luxury, despite a state of siege (1.21-22). Amasis, faced with a lack of respect from his subjects makes a religious statue out of an erstwhile golden footbath. He uses it to point the moral to his subordinates, that like the footbath he too has changed his form and is now worthy of veneration as king (2.172).

Such figures do not succeed because they are nicer or better people than others; as Legrand suggests, their singleminded ruthlessness is often quite unattractive. In one important respect, however, they resemble the savants and this seems to be the key to their effectiveness in action. The trickster figures know that they cannot get what they want through open means; by looking at the elements of the situation carefully, they find a way to exploit its possibilities to their own advantage. In this sense alone they are free from the delusion that blinds most conventional political leaders. Many of the female actors in the *Histories* succeed in attaining their goals by exploiting the false assumptions of their male opponents.[13] Males too, even those like

[13] See my "Women and Culture in Herodotus' *Histories*," in H. Foley, ed., *Reflections of Women in Antiquity* (New York 1981) 105-107.

Cleomenes and Themistocles who do have political power of a conventional sort, achieve by finesse what they could not have achieved by open means. They are rewarded not for their morals or their character, but for a certain grim intellectual realism that finds expression in unconventional action. Where the savant-advisors understand the world but often cannot convince others of the relevance of their observations, the trickster figures express their understanding of the realities of the situation in action; because they see the situation as it is, they generally succeed in their plans. They exploit the advantages of the situation and the conventional assumptions of the other actors for their own advantage.[14]

Thus Herodotus' implicit model of the relation between practical knowledge and political action is rather complex. He continues to accept the archaic belief that *hubris* leads to *atē*. The *hubris* that interests Herodotus, however, is very much an intellectual one, and he himself is not so much interested in its theological ramifications as in its sociology. There are facts about the physical world and about human behavior that Herodotus believes it perilous to ignore. Events, *ta genomena*, occur as the result of a complex interaction of a large number of such facts. Figures like Solon and Hecataeus or, in a different style, Themistocles, Amasis, and Artemisia act in accordance with this basic truth. Because they take the trouble to look closely at the realities that surround them, they understand events as more conventional political actors, however well-meaning or pious, do not.

Thucydides' treatment of the relation between practical knowledge and action is very different. First, there are no savants in Thucydides, no wise advisors who understand reality more clearly because of their general interest in facts about the world and the men who inhabit it. In part this difference is the result of Thucydides' choice of topic. Thucydides describes a political world largely dominated by the assumptions of Athenian, that is, democratic politics. As Pericles puts it in the Funeral Oration, in such a context everyone is a political actor; those who maintain a detached attitude toward events are simply

---

[14] One should perhaps talk about isolated instances of trickster behavior rather than of tricksters as fixed personalities in Herodotus. A number of Herodotean figures lose their trickster qualities in the course of their careers. Darius, for instance, begins as a trickster but later misjudges events like a conventional ruler; Cleomenes ends by becoming mad. H. Immerwahr comments on usurpers as trickster figures and on *apatē* as a standard aspect of Herodotean warfare; he also points out that trickster figures seem to accept good advice more readily than other actors: *Form and Thought in Herodotus* (Cleveland 1966) 170, 167, 243, 224, 277.

irrelevant (2.40.2). There is a more sinister side to this fact as well. Thucydides calls war a *biaios didaskalos* (3.82.2). In Thucydides' judgment, no city and no individual within the city remains unaffected by war's power brutally to transform the language and behavior of Greek politics.[15]

Thus Thucydides does not believe in the usefulness or even in the possibility of a political knowledge divorced from the exercise of personal and civic ambition. As the Athenians say at the first assembly at Sparta, all men are driven by fear, honor, and advantage (1.76). Those who believe otherwise Thucydides shows to be in the grip of a dangerous illusion.[16] He pities the victims in his *History*, those who suffer terribly at the hands of their enemies. But when, like the Plataeans, the Melians, or Nicias at Syracuse, men look to the altruism or detachment of others to save them from the consequences of their own misjudgment, they suffer because they have engaged in wishful thinking. Like Herodotus, Thucydides believes that effective action requires the abandonment of false assumptions about the world. One of the false notions he appears to reject, however, is the model of the disengaged savant. There are no knowledgeable onlookers in Thucydides' *History*.

Another important contrast exists in Thucydides' treatment of political engagement. Thucydides does not distinguish between conventional political leaders and trickster figures. Despite clear differences in effectiveness, all of Thucydides' actors are intense, intelligent, and serious in the pursuit of their own political ends. Where only a handful of individuals in Herodotus deliver serious symbouleutic speeches, Thucydides allows all of the actors in his account to speak in a thoroughly Thucydidean mode, using the best arguments they know in defense of their positions. Even figures like Cleon or Athenagoras, whom Thucydides shows to misunderstand the nature of events, argue clearly and cogently for their own points of view (3.37-40; 6.36-40).[17]

[15] For the most recent and fullest statement of this theme, see P. Pouncey (above, note 3).

[16] P. Shorey, "On the Implicit Ethics and Psychology of Thucydides," *TAPA* 24 (1893) 66-88, calls this aspect of the *History* "intellectualism," "ethical positivism," and "moral insensibility." W. R. Connor, "A Post Modernist Thucydides?," *CJ* 72 (1977) 295, points out that a number of recent studies have rectified this earlier view of Thucydides as an amoral scientist. See especially Thucydides' sense of tragic pathos, in H.-P. Stahl, *Thukydides: Die Stellung des Menschen im Geschichtlichen Prozess* (München 1966).

[17] P. Huart, *Le vocabulaire de l'analyse psychologique dans l'oeuvre de Thucydide* (Paris 1968) 166 and 242-246, remarks that Thucydides depicts everyone as engaged in rational calculation except Thracians and crowds in the grip of emotion.

Connected to this is the fact that Thucydides is not interested in the Solon leitmotif, the brevity and unpredictability of human life and the likelihood that political actors will profoundly misunderstand the limitations placed by the gods on human understanding and power. On the rare occasions when this topic is raised, Thucydides' treatment of it is Homeric rather than archaic. As Pericles repeatedly tells the Athenians, the fact that man is mortal means that the effort to achieve must be that much greater, the determination to win what one can more unremitting (1.144.3; 2.42-43; 2.64.3). Political actors in Thucydides often incorrectly assess the complexities of their situation. They fail to see the extent to which their own desires and fears have distorted their judgment; sometimes they fail to account for the large role that *tuchē* plays in human affairs.[18] But Thucydides does not criticize them for *hubris*, or for assuming that their control over events is greater than it is. The complexity of the causal connections established in the narrative rather emphasizes the difficulty of understanding events when one is in the midst of them. Individual actors (though not always groups) make serious arguments; even if the outcome is disastrous, Thucydides is concerned to show that their stance was an intelligible one. He clarifies the reasons why they thought as they did.[19]

A fourth, and final, difference in his treatment of the relation between knowledge and political action is perhaps the most important of all. Thucydides characterizes a small number of political actors as *xunetoi*, intelligent.[20] The *xunetoi* in Thucydides' *History* accept and indeed articulate Thucydides' own belief that self-interest is the mainspring of all human action. Hermocrates announces, of Athenian imperialism: "I do not blame those who are resolved to rule, but those who show an even greater readiness to submit" (4.61). Brasidas echoes this sentiment: "Straightforward aggression has a certain justification in the strength provided by fortune" (4.86). Diodotus makes a similar

---

[18] See L. Edmunds, *Chance and Intelligence in Thucydides* (Cambridge, Mass. 1975).

[19] See R. Aron, "Thucydide et le récit des événements," *History and Theory* 1 (1961) 110: "...la décision résulte d'un calcul. Cette décision nous paraît rationnelle, même quand elle n'est pas donnée par Thucydide comme la seule possible, elle nous paraît intelligible même quand elle se révèle finalement erronée."

[20] Individuals are called especially intelligent in 1.79.2; 4.81.2; 6.72.2; 8.27.5; 8.68.4. Individuals are singled out for admiration in comparable terms in 1.138.2-3; 2.15.2; 2.65.5-9 and 13; 6.54.5; 8.68.1. See H. Westlake, *Individuals in Thucydides* (Cambridge 1968) 5-15, for a survey of Thucydides' explicit judgments on ability and character.

point in the context of city politics. He replies to Cleon's allegations of personal opportunism that it is really immaterial whether an individual reaps private benefits from advocating a particular course of action. If he can persuade his fellow citizens that the city will benefit too, his private affairs are of no consequence (3.42.2-43.1).

The *xunetoi* in Thucydides are not manipulators, like the Herodotean tricksters. Like the Herodotean figures, however, they are distinguished from other political actors in the *History* by a certain intellectual independence. They act according to their chosen course of judgment, even in the face of disapproval and opposition about them. Pericles resists the Spartans' claims to moderation and leads Athens into war because he believes that war with the Peloponnese is inevitable and that Athens can win such a war (1.141). After the plague has devastated Athens, he remains unshaken in his convictions and reprimands the Athenians for their inconstancy of judgment (2.60-64). Phrynichus refuses to risk the remnants of the Athenian fleet in a battle that he thinks unwise, despite pressure from other Athenian generals. He also sees through the fantasies of his fellow oligarchs, being the only one to perceive the nature of Alcibiades' political motivations and the true relations that prevail between Athens and the subject allies (8.27; 8.48). Brasidas incurs jealousy from other Spartan leaders. He makes his career by staying as far away from Sparta itself as possible; he is an anomaly both as a good speaker (for a Spartan) and as a brilliantly innovative general (4.81; 4.84; 4.108.6-7). Themistocles, of course, represents this independence of opinion and trust in his own judgment in their most extreme form. He cynically uses the time of his visit as an honored guest at Sparta to rebuild the walls in Athens, despite Spartan opposition (1.90-91). In exile he is under no illusion that either the Spartans or the Athenians will remember past benefits, and he flees to an escape already prepared in Persia. Almost our last glimpse of him shows him learning the Persian language and customs so as to be independent of others when he comes to court (1.138).

The *xunetoi* in Thucydides do not always achieve what they have undertaken. Chance enters into their lives and disrupts their calculations just as it does those of everyone else. Brasidas dies at Amphipolis; Phrynichus is assassinated and the revolution engineered by him fails; Hermocrates, the architect of the Sicilian victory over Athens, is at length exiled and powerless; even Pericles does not foresee the plague and his own death two years into the war (5.10; 8.92; 8.85.3; 2.64.1).

But in one very important sense, Thucydides believes that the political decisions of the *xunetoi* are sounder and generally more secure in their results than those of other men. Like Thucydides himself, the *xunetoi* understand that there is a distinction between short-term and long-term political accomplishment. Themistocles and Pericles bring Athens a half-century of greatness unlike that attained by any other Greek state; Brasidas and Hermocrates permanently destroy the forward momentum of the Athenian empire and critically cripple Athens in the war. Even the Athenian oligarchs achieve something noteworthy that later events do not obscure or eradicate, "for it was difficult, about a century after the tyrants had been deposed, to deprive the Athenian people of its freedom..." (8.68.4). The *xunetoi* in the *History* of Thucydides gain for themselves and their cities the *doxa aieimnēstos* that Pericles defines as the only lasting human accomplishment (2.64.5). They do so because they share Thucydides' own understanding of the workings of power and the nature of real self-interest, and they have the strength of mind to pursue their own goals despite the obstacles set in their way by others or by the chances of war.

Both Herodotus and Thucydides believe that political knowledge does exist. For both authors, people are more successful when they act according to this knowledge, less successful when they do not. But the two authors define the basic elements of this practical knowledge very differently. For Herodotus, it is an important truth that human knowledge of the world is always partial and provisional; by definition it is always based on incomplete evidence, as Solon makes clear to Croesus. The objects — cups, bowls, maps, and so forth — whose reality people habitually misinterpret express this truth in the narrative of events. The world and the causal connections that exist within it are much more complex than most political leaders imagine. Within this general pessimistic assessment those individuals are more successful in action who understand this fact and so take the trouble to understand as much as they can of the situation confronting them. On the rare occasions when a leader accepts the advice of a savant, the outcome is favorable; when a trickster manipulates an opponent's faulty assumptions, he (or she) almost always succeeds.

Thucydides understands the relation between knowledge and political action very differently. This is partly because he defines successful achievement more modestly than Herodotus does. The truth expressed by Herodotus' Solon is for him a mere truism; Solon's standards of success are irrelevant. Thucydides admires men who demonstrate the capacity to formulate realistic political goals within a limited context and to implement these goals in action. A number of actors he depicts as knowledgeable and capable men — genuine political leaders in a way Herodotus permits no one to be. Thucydides understands that man is mortal; because the world is too complex and *tuchē* too pervasive, even the *xunetoi* do not always succeed in their undertakings. But Thucydides adds a final element to his definition of successful political action; the achievement of a *doxa aieimnēstos* is the mark of ultimate success, and its achievement is not necessarily contingent upon short-term success. The capacity to keep this fact in mind is, for Thucydides, the element that distinguishes the really intelligent political actors from their fellows.

It is time now to return to the second aspect of the self-consciousness of history as a new invention in the fifth century B.C.; that is, the author's obligation to tell his audience who he is, and what kind of stance he intends to take toward the narrative he is presenting. As we have seen, history exists as a genre because Herodotus and Thucydides define their tasks in similar ways. But their basic stances as authors toward their material differ considerably. Each has a notion of authorial integrity that he scrupulously follows in the text. In each, there are obvious parallels to be drawn between the author's presentation of his own role and that of the most intelligent individuals in his narrative. Thus Herodotus' authorial stance bears affinities to the position of the savants and trickster figures in his text. Like the savants he defines his own role as that of an observer and an investigator rather than as a participant. He stands apart from the *logoi* that constitute his *Histories* and scrutinizes them. This is evident even in the way he writes the first sentence: "This is the display of the investigation of Herodotus the Halicarnassian." Moreover, just as the trickster figures divine the true meaning of physical objects that deceive others, Herodotus presents himself as someone who knows how to question the surface appearance of the *logoi* and penetrate as much as possible to the reality that they often disguise.[21]

Thucydides, on the other hand, adopts a position similar to that of his *xunetoi*. Like them, he accepts the notion of a political knowledge closely coupled with practical action. He depicts himself both as an

---

[21] This topic forms the thesis of my forthcoming study (above, note 3).

actor inside the narrative of events and as the writer of the *logos* he gives us. He does not, like Herodotus, stand apart from the narrative and present it as a report of his investigations. He states rather that what follows is his own *logos*; he is its author: "Thucydides the Athenian wrote up the war of the Peloponnesians and the Athenians." Apart from two brief passages that serve as methodological introductions, Thucydides does not interrupt the narrative to give information about the process of research and composition. The *logos* is *his* voice and thus represents his own best judgment about the meaning of events.

This same difference in attitude extends to the two authors' treatment of themselves as historical figures. Although Herodotus is lavish with information about the difficulty of being a *histōr* of *logoi*, he is quite unforthcoming about himself as an individual. It is irrelevant to his role as an investigator. Thucydides, on the other hand, talks about his own role in the war he recounts. More importantly, the very narrative of events forms an ongoing political dialogue, in which he, the *xunetoi*, and even the other individual speakers all participate. As Aron has noted, what emerges may be read as a contemporary intellectual history of the Peloponnesian War. All of the participants, including Thucydides himself, speak with the same vocabulary and out of the same basic assumptions about politics and political activity. Each voice in turn adds the essential logic of its viewpoint.[22]

Traditionally, the difference between these two authorial stances has been explained in the context of a gradually developing self-consciousness in the genre. According to this argument, Herodotus, closer in time to the origins of the genre in epic and travellers' tales, has not yet understood the seriousness of the task in which he is engaged. Perhaps he is the butt of Thucydides' charge, writing ἐπὶ τὸ προσαγωγότερον τῇ ἀκροάσει ἢ ἀληθέστερον (1.21.1). When judged by Thucydides' standards, Herodotus' detachment does at times seem frivolous and dismissive of the overriding need for accuracy that Thucydides articulates. But if the model for the relation between knowledge and action which I have argued in each author's narrative of events is correct, this argument obscures and trivializes the differences between Herodotus and Thucydides as authors. It is not a question of seriousness; as I hope to have shown, they have two

---

[22] Aron (above, note 19). See also the more detailed arguments of J. Finley, "The Origins of Thucydides' Style," *Three Essays on Thucydides* (Cambridge, Mass. 1967) 55-117.

different visions of what knowledge is, and how as authors to be in a position to obtain and express it. Knowledge is for Herodotus the preserve of those who stand apart and look; thus he presents himself as a detached and skeptical observer of the *logoi* that he studies. Thucydides does not believe in such a detachment. He presents the narrative as his own considered judgment on the meaning of events. It is politically engaged in another more fundamental sense as well. Thucydides believes that his own *History* is itself the best guarantee that the *xunetoi* within the account will receive the *doxa aieimnēstos* that their actions have deserved.[23]

Each author has a vision of how reflective men can operate in the world of events with understanding; each reproduces this sense of things in his own presentation of himself as an author in his text. If this argument is correct, some final arguments can be made about the social context in which Herodotus and Thucydides began to write history. The most obvious is the relevance of their two postures to what we know of their personal biographies. If any of the ancient evidence can be trusted, Herodotus knew exile at an early age and spent a portion of his middle years as a political outsider observing the deterioration in relations between Athens and the Peloponnese. It is difficult not to read the cry of the Persian before the battle of Plataea as Herodotus' own: "The most hateful of all of men's sorrows is this, thinking many things, to control none" (9.16.5). Thucydides' experience, on the other hand, was not that of an onlooker but of a citizen. His exile occurred only in middle age, and even in exile he retained the perceptions and intuitions of one who from the inside knows and cares about the complexities of democratic politics. These interested him in a way that they did not interest Herodotus, and his history reflects his sense of their importance.

So much is likely to be true. But if this point is given too much weight, it becomes a mere truism, a sophisticated version of the commonplace that the writing of every historian reflects his own experience of the world. More interesting is the relation between each author's sociology of knowledge and his role in the intellectual movement we call the first sophistic, or the Greek enlightenment. Here I can only suggest some potential lines of inquiry. The Herodotus I have tried to describe here bears a strong resemblance to some of the figures

---

[23] See further, A. Parry, "Thucydides' Historical Perspective," *YCS* 22 (1972) 47-61.

from the first generation of sophistic thinkers. Like Protagoras and Socrates in Plato's *Protagoras*, Herodotus struggles intellectually to understand and define the role of traditional and oral knowledge in a culture that is becoming literate.[24] Herodotus has felt the seductive power of oral *logoi* about the past, and his attitude toward them is complex. On the one hand, he wants to preserve them as the only record available of past events. He knows, however, that he cannot simply record them. Like Protagoras, Gorgias, and Socrates, he is concerned with the problem of language and its relation to knowledge; he records the *logoi* but also studies them with the analytical tools necessary to dispel their uncanny powers of persuasion. Thus his *Histories* are intended not just to be a record of what the *logoi* say; they are also a demonstration (*apodexis*) of how one goes about investigating the mixture of truth and falsehood that *logoi* from the past contain. Herodotus' detachment remains his best guarantee that he has preserved the integrity of his investigatory role.

Thucydides, perhaps half a generation later, is not concerned with these issues. *Logoi* do not hold for him a semiautonomous status as things in themselves. Thucydides is interested rather in the psychology that produces political discourse; he studies men and institutions and uses his own words to present his results. Because Herodotus has dispelled the power of *logoi* to seduce their hearers into uncritically accepting their version of events, Thucydides can treat the written word as a difficult but essentially stable and enduring medium through which to communicate his judgments on men and events.

---

[24] The relation of the narrative procedures of both Herodotus and Thucydides to the intellectual concerns of the first sophistic needs further study. For Thucydides, see F. Solmsen, *Intellectual Experiments of the Greek Enlightenment* (Princeton 1975); for Herodotus, see A. Dihle, "Herodot und die Sophistik," *Philologus* 106 (1962) 207-220. See J. Evans, *Herodotus* (Boston 1982) 145-153 for Herodotus' use of oral traditions. I would like to thank M.H. Jameson and R.S. Stroud for their helpful comments on an earlier draft of this paper.

1001 Iranian Nights: History and Fiction in Xenophon's Cyropaedia

STEVEN W. HIRSCH
Tufts University

This paper, which concerns itself with one of the more curious pieces of literature which have come down to us from classical antiquity — the *Cyropaedia* of Xenophon — is written in that spirit of respect for the intelligence and integrity of the ancient authors which has always characterized the writing and teaching of Toni Raubitschek, to whom this volume is dedicated.

Xenophon, as is well known, was an Athenian of aristocratic family whose adult life spanned the first half of the fourth century B.C. Student of Socrates, participant in the unsuccessful revolt of the Persian prince Cyrus, mercenary commander, exile, friend of the Spartan king Agesilaus, gentleman farmer and litterateur, he experienced more of the world than is granted to most men.

Xenophon nevertheless is a much maligned figure who has been out of favor with students of Greek literature and history in recent times. Somewhere it has been said that he was "a better philosopher than Thucydides, a better historian than Plato," by which it was meant that he was thoroughly mediocre in all his endeavors. Certainly, no one would presume to claim that he was the equal of such intellectual giants as Thucydides and Plato. But Xenophon was a more interesting and creative personality than is usually allowed. Indeed, in certain respects he shows greater enlightenment than his more brilliant and famous contemporaries. For one thing, he had overcome typical Greek prejudices towards barbarians and had developed a balanced and respectful attitude towards Persia,[1] that vast empire whose power and pretensions cast a shadow across the Greek consciousness throughout the classical era. In his political theorizing Xenophon is able to do what Plato and Aristotle cannot — to envision a stage of political development beyond the independent Greek *polis*. In this, as in other respects, he foreshadows the Hellenistic age ushered in by Alexander the Great a quarter century after his death. Finally, he wrote books on a wide range of topics, historical, philosophical and technical. Here he was an innovator who was not afraid to cross traditional genre lines, and who created, or participated in the early development of, several new literary genres — memoir in the *Anabasis*, philosophic dialogue in the *Memorabilia*, biography in the *Agesilaus*.

Perhaps the most difficult to categorize of all his works is the *Cyropaedia*. The title, Κύρου παιδεία, means "The Education of Cyrus," and is nominally the story of Cyrus the Great, the Iranian king who founded the Persian Empire in the mid-sixth century B.C. But the eight books of the *Cyropaedia* amount to far more than the education of Cyrus, unless education is taken in its widest sense as the experience and knowledge gathered during a lifetime. The work begins with the ancestry and birth of Cyrus, and gives ample coverage to his boyhood and education. Glossing over his years as a teenager and young adult, it concentrates on his conquests and the initial provisions which he made for administration of the new empire which he had won. It then skips over the rest of his reign until it reaches his last days and his deathbed political testament to friends and heirs.

In the preface Xenophon makes the following claim:

> Thus, as we meditated on this analogy, we were inclined to conclude that for man, as he is constituted, it is easier to rule over any and all other creatures than to rule over men. But when we reflected that there was one Cyrus, the Persian, who reduced to obedience a vast number of men and cities and nations, we were then compelled to change our opinion and decide that to rule men might be a task neither impossible nor even difficult, if one should only go about it in an intelligent manner... Believing this man to be deserving of all admiration, we have

---

[1] Steven W. Hirsch, *The Friendship of the Barbarians: Xenophon and the Persian Empire* (forthcoming in 1985).

therefore investigated who he was in his origin, what natural endowments he possessed, and what sort of education he had enjoyed, that he so greatly excelled in governing men. Accordingly, what we have found out or think we know concerning him we shall now endeavor to present. (*Cyropaedia* 1.1.3; 1.1.6)[2]

The reader is urged to keep in mind that, on Xenophon's own testimony, the *Cyropaedia* is an investigation of how Cyrus conquered and ruled his empire.

Despite Xenophon's explicit statement of purpose, there has never been a consensus on the question — "What is the *Cyropaedia?*" There are almost as many opinions as there are commentators on such fundamental issues as the genre of the work, its purpose and its inspiration. This is because it does not fit neatly into any established literary genre, ancient or modern.

What can be said, however, is that the majority of classical scholars have never been able to give any serious regard to the historical setting of the *Cyropaedia*, that is, the Old Persia of Cyrus the Great. To quote a recent study of Xenophon:

> Xenophon's choice of subject need not, therefore, be taken as an indication of some new cosmopolitanism, nor a reflection of his own travels abroad, especially since a Persian ingredient in the *Kyroupaideia* is little more than a flavoring.[3]

For most classicists, the Persian context of the *Cyropaedia* is mere exotic decoration and of no real significance. They prefer to see it as a thoroughly Greek work which has been transferred to a fairy-tale "Persian" setting. Moreover, they imply that Xenophon simply invented most of the alleged "events" in the career of his Cyrus. It follows that, for them, the work is worth little as a source of information on Persian history, culture or institutions, nor can one gain from it any insights into the attitude of fourth century Greeks towards Persia.

---

[2] Translation of Walter Miller, *Xenophon: Cyropaedia* (London and Cambridge, Massachusetts 1914).

[3] W.E. Higgins, *Xenophon the Athenian* (Albany 1977) 44. J. Joel Farber, *Xenophon's Theory of Kingship* (dissertation Yale, 1959) xiv-xix, summarized the wildly divergent suggestions of classicists about the genre and/or meaning of the *Cyropaedia*. Few seem to take the Persian elements of the *Cyropaedia* seriously. Two noteworthy exceptions, which were not available when Farber wrote, are Joan M. Todd, *Persian 'Paedia' and Greek 'Historia': An Interpretation of the Cyropaedia of Xenophon, Book One* (dissertation Pittsburgh 1968), and Wolfgang Knauth, *Das altiranische Fürstenideal von Xenophon bis Ferdousi* (Wiesbaden 1975).

On the other hand, many Orientalists who are concerned with the civilization of ancient Iran have taken a very different view. For them the *Cyropaedia* has long been a major source of information concerning the history and institutions of the Persian Empire.

In light of these two fundamentally antithetical approaches to the work,[4] it is a matter of obvious importance to determine the nature of the *Cyropaedia*. Is it history, is it fiction, or is it something in between? The answer to this question will dictate the extent to which, and the way in which, the historian is entitled to make use of the *Cyropaedia*. And insofar as the *Cyropaedia* was widely read in antiquity[5] and had considerable impact on the evolution of a number of literary genres, it should be a matter of interest, not just to the historian of ancient Persia, but also to the intellectual historian who is concerned with the development of Greek thought.

To understand the nature of the *Cyropaedia* and the purposes of the author, it is essential to grasp the role of Persia in the work. Herein lies the key to the *Cyropaedia*. The traditional view of classicists, as has been said, is to minimize the significance of the Persian historical and cultural context. But there are a number of reasons for questioning this traditional view. In the first place, it begs the question to assert that Xenophon's choice of a Persian setting is of no particular importance. This issue deserves to be examined with an open mind. One must ask why Xenophon has chosen a Persian king and allegedly Persian models of education, ethics, leadership and administration to express his ideals. The question takes on added interest if the Greeks of the fourth century were really as contemptuous of Persian "barbarians" as is commonly maintained, for these same Greeks were the audience for whom Xenophon wrote.

In the second place, those who insist that the authentically Persian features in the *Cyropaedia* are few and inconsequential are simply mistaken. Indeed, the *Cyropaedia* contains numerous facts about the

---

[4] This divergence in approach was remarked upon by Farber (above, note 3) xix, with a brief bibliography of Orientalists, admittedly from an earlier generation, who quarried the *Cyropaedia* for data on Persia. Orientalists continue to have respect for the *Cyropaedia*, e.g. Mary Boyce, *A History of Zoroastrianism* vol. II (Leiden 1982) 211-16. Classicists continue to minimize its historical value, most recently J.M. Cook, *The Persian Empire* (New York 1983) 20-21.

[5] Brief treatment by Farber (above, note 3) vi-xiv. Full coverage in Karl Münscher, *Xenophon in der griechisch-römischen Literatur* (Philologus Supplementband XIII, Heft II [1920]).

Persian Empire, its history, culture, institutions and peoples. Some can be confirmed elsewhere in Greek and Oriental sources, while others are at least quite plausible. Xenophon claims that many of the customs and institutions of the elder Cyrus' day are still in force in Persia in his own time.[6] He also claims to have done research and to have had access to Oriental songs and legends.[7] Moreover, Orientalists have detected stories and motifs in the *Cyropaedia* which recur in different contexts in the *Shahnama* and other Persian literature based on early oral tradition.[8] Consequently, the investigator of the *Cyropaedia* must ask himself why Xenophon has gone to the trouble of discovering and reporting this wealth of data about Persia.

In the third place, it must be realized that the *Cyropaedia* is about the acquisition and administration, not of a *polis*, but of an empire. Some commentators explain that Xenophon was deeply disturbed by the instability of city-state governments and the incessant warfare within and between the Greek communities during his lifetime, and that this prompted him to a discourse on government in the *Cyropaedia*. Thus, the *Cyropaedia* is supposed to be seen as prescribing some sort of solution to the problems of the Greek *polis*.[9] Once again, those who espouse this view seem to be proceeding from a set of *a priori* assumptions about what the attitude and interests of Xenophon, as a patriotic fourth century Greek, ought to have been.

Indeed, many of Xenophon's contemporaries were concerned with the problems of the Greek city-state. Plato in the *Republic* and the *Laws* and Aristotle in the *Politics* gave much deep thought to the nature of the *polis*, and each offered his vision of the ideal community. In both cases the emphasis is on the structure of the state. However, the comparison with Plato and Aristotle only serves to point up the differences in Xenophon's approach. Not only is Xenophon talking

---

[6] These instances are usually marked by some variant of the phrase ἔτι καὶ νῦν. E. Delebecque, *Essai sur la vie de Xénophon* (Paris 1957) 395-96, gives a partial list of these passages.

[7] Research—1.1. Reference to stories and songs about Cyrus to be found among the barbarians—1.2.1; 1.4.25; 1.4.27; 8.5.28; 8.6.16; 8.6.20.

[8] Arthur E. Christensen, *Les gestes des rois dans les traditions de l'Iran antique* (Paris 1936) 122-35. Boyce (above, note 4) 211-16, who assumes that much of what Xenophon describes in the *Cyropaedia* is based on his own experience with the younger Cyrus, finds Xenophon a reliable reporter of Zoroastrian practices.

[9] E.g. Delebecque (above, note 6) 387, who argues that in the 350s Xenophon wanted to advise the Athenians on the critical issues of the day.

about a much larger and more complex political entity, that is, an empire extending over vast distances and comprising many different peoples, with all the problems of administration that this must entail, but he also focuses not so much on political structures as on the character of the individual ruler. Could he really have been prompted to this meditation by a desire to solve the problems of (for the sake of example) the contemporary Athenian democracy?

In fact, things had not been going entirely well for the Persian Empire either in the fourth century, what with the secession of Egypt, the attempted coup d'état of Cyrus the younger, and revolts of Cypriots, Phoenicians and disaffected Persian satraps. One should not dismiss out of hand the possibility that Xenophon has been prompted to these reflections by the problems of contemporary Persia. At any rate, one must ask—"Why has Xenophon concerned himself with the problems facing an *individual* who seeks to rule, not a city-state, but an *empire*?"

The foregoing considerations raise doubts about the prevailing assumption that the Persian context and the authentically Persian elements of the *Cyropaedia* are superficial and of little real moment. Xenophon obviously had a keen interest in, and ample knowledge about, Persia. It is my contention that the *Cyropaedia* is much more "Persian" in inspiration than is usually conceded. In order to establish this contention, it will be necessary to consider, first, the character of the *Cyropaedia*, by which I mean its genre, the sources to which Xenophon had access and the way in which he used them. Then we will take up the problem of the Persian setting, and I will suggest a number of reasons why Xenophon may have chosen to set his account in the Old Persia of Cyrus the Great. Finally, we will briefly take up the question of how reliable the *Cyropaedia* is as a source of information on the history, culture, and institutions of ancient Persia. Only from the vantage point provided by such a survey can one fairly evaluate the true position of the *Cyropaedia* on that elusive boundary between history and fiction.

There is, as has been said, little agreement among commentators about the genre of the *Cyropaedia*. Perhaps there is no single, simple answer, since here, as elsewhere, Xenophon was apparently willing to cross traditional genre lines. Nevertheless, certain things can be said. The starting point must be Xenophon's own prefatory statement that he is concerned with the question of how one may govern that most problematic of creatures — Man — and that Cyrus' success in this enterprise makes him a fruitful subject for investigation.[10] On Xenophon's own testimony, the *Cyropaedia* is to be an investigation of how Cyrus conquered and ruled his empire. In accordance with this design, Xenophon focuses on certain episodes in Cyrus' life — youth, conquests, initial consolidation of power and last moments — and virtually ignores the rest of a long life. Events from the past have been selected, and segments of Cyrus' life emphasized, largely because they illuminate the matter of what kind of ruler Cyrus had been. This selection allows Xenophon to expatiate upon the early signs of Cyrus' outstanding nature, the program of education which molded his character, the manner in which he carried out his conquests, his initial provisions for administration of the new empire, and his death-bed political testament. Thus, while it may contain much historical and biographical material, the *Cyropaedia* is neither history nor biography. A comprehensive and continuous treatment of the full career of Cyrus, such as would be expected in either a history of Old Persia or a biography of Cyrus, is not attempted and was surely never contemplated.

In light of Xenophon's statement of purpose and the contents of the work, it can, perhaps, be characterized as a didactic work on the subjects of education, values, military science, and political administration, drawing upon the example of Cyrus for its paradigmatic value and in order to provide a cohesive and entertaining framework for the instructional material. Such a formulation is safe enough and would probably win general approbation, but it does not tackle the fundamental issue of historicity. As was seen earlier, many classical scholars regard the framework of plot and setting as largely, or entirely, fictional, and believe that Xenophon invented most of the story line and drew his intellectual inspiration from Greek societies such as Sparta.[11] To assert this is to ignore Xenophon's twin claims that he means to examine the career of the historical Cyrus for the illumination which it may provide on the problem of good government and that he is going to relate what he had discovered as a result of his researches.

[10] See above, pages 66-67.
[11] E.g. Donald Kagan, *The Great Dialogue: A History of Greek Political Thought from Homer to Polybius* (New York 1965) 150.

At this juncture, we need to consider the sources of information on Old Persia which were available to Xenophon. They fall into three major categories. First, Greek books. Although he does not cite Herodotus by name anywhere, it is highly probable that he was familiar with Herodotus' *Histories*. There are strong similarities between Xenophon's and Herodotus' accounts of Cyrus' capture of Sardis and Babylon. Furthermore, Xenophon's story of the interview between Cyrus and Croesus, the captured king of Lydia, virtually proves his familiarity with the Herodotean version, for his alteration of the Herodotean account of these events amounts to an implicit criticism of Herodotus' treatment of the role of Delphi (*Cyropaedia* 7.2.9-28).[12] That he had read Ctesias' *Persica* is proven by his citation of it in the *Anabasis* (1.8.26). It is reasonable to assume that he made some use of Ctesias for the *Cyropaedia*.[13] As will be seen later, there are strong similarities between his and Ctesias' accounts of the death of Cyrus. Xenophon probably also made use of other Greek historical works which have not survived, or whose remains are too fragmentary to permit a firm connection to be established.[14]

Barbarian oral tradition constitutes a second category of source material. Xenophon occasionally cites the stories and songs about Cyrus to be found among the barbarians.[15] Clearly Cyrus had become a figure of legend among the peoples of the Near East.[16] Herodotus claimed to be aware of four different versions of the birth of Cyrus and many tales of his death (1.95; 1.214), and this process of mythifying will have gone that much further by Xenophon's time.[17]

[12] Karl-August Riemann, *Das Herodoteische Geschichtswerk in der Antike* (Munich 1967) 20-27; E. Lefevre, "Die Frage nach dem βίος εὐδαίμων: Die Begegnung zwischen Kyros und Kroisos bei Xenophon," *Hermes* 99 (1971) 283-96.

[13] See below, note 17.

[14] H.R. Breitenbach, *Xenophon von Athen* (Stuttgart 1966) 1709, suggests Dionysius of Miletus, Hellanicus, Xanthus and Charon of Lampsacus as possible sources. For a discussion of Xenophon's possible debt to Antisthenes, who wrote a dialogue entitled *Cyrus*, see Ragnar Höistad, *Cynic Hero and Cynic King* (Uppsala 1948) 77-94.

[15] See above, note 7.

[16] See Robert Drews, "Sargon, Cyrus and Mesopotamian Folk History," *Journal of Near Eastern Studies* 33 (1974) 387-93.

[17] Joan M. Bigwood, *Ctesias of Cnidus* (dissertation Harvard 1964) 186, notes that Ctesias devoted five books to tales of Cyrus the Great. This gives an indication of the extent of the traditions about Cyrus which were available to Xenophon, whether in Ctesias or in the native tradition.

Xenophon presumably picked up such stories in the course of his travels in the Persian Empire, first as a member of the entourage of the younger Cyrus and later as a commander of Greek mercenaries.

Xenophon's experiences in the Persian Empire are also integral to the third category of evidence. Obviously he could draw upon what he had seen and learned first-hand in the course of his travels. There is ample evidence that Xenophon tended to read back into the past certain Persian practices of his own day. He frequently marks this by employing some variant of the phrase ἔτι καὶ νῦν — "and still today..."[18]

Thus Xenophon claims to have done research and he had access to a variety of sources. We may have our doubts about the historicity of Herodotus' and Ctesias' accounts of the career of Cyrus and about the veracity of the oral traditions circulating among the barbarians. And, in some cases, Xenophon may be mistaken in assuming that a contemporary Persian institution or custom was in existence already in Cyrus' day. But what is most important, for present purposes, is that Xenophon drew upon sources of information which he considered, and had every reason to consider, to be of some value.

It is fair to assume that Xenophon, like Herodotus before him, often had a number of versions of a story from which to choose, especially in the case of a now-legendary figure such as Cyrus. Sometimes he takes over a version which we know to be derived from Herodotus or Ctesias. In these cases there is no problem. At other times he gives a different account which is not attested elsewhere. Critics tend to point to these cases as examples of how Xenophon is prone to fabricate stories at will. However, later in this paper we will examine several instances in which the chance survival of outside evidence guarantees that the authority of Xenophon is to be preferred to that of Herodotus.[19] It is, therefore, methodologically unsound simply to presume that Xenophon has invented any story for which independent confirmation has not chanced to survive into modern times.

Why does Xenophon choose the particular version which he reports in a given case? This brings us back to the problem of genre and purpose. If the *Cyropaedia* is a didactic work, then his principle of selection is most likely the suitability of a given version to his didactic purposes. With numerous traditions about Cyrus in circulation,

18 See above, note 6.
19 See below, pages 80-83.

Xenophon was in a position to choose the ones which best enabled him to illustrate those qualities of character and intellect which he felt were most important in a leader and ruler. There is no indication that he has submitted the material which he gathered to the kind of rigorous critical scrutiny which a Thucydides would have demanded. After all, a precise reconstruction of the past is not Xenophon's avowed goal. However, there is a meaningful difference between spontaneous invention of stories, of which Xenophon is so frequently accused, and the selective use of authentic traditions about the past.[20]

To this point I have been arguing that we should take Xenophon at his word when he claims to have drawn upon authentic traditions about Cyrus and Old Persia in order to explore the problem of government. But how are we to account for the fact that Xenophon has chosen a Persian setting for the framework of his didactic treatise? It is a choice that is, in many ways, surprising, especially if one accepts the standard pronouncements about the hostility towards Persia of Xenophon and his Greek contemporaries. Some scholars dodge the apparent paradox by claiming that the Persian setting is a matter of little real significance — a literary fancy and nothing more — and need not be taken seriously. They confidently explain that the distance in space and time of Cyrus' Old Persia removed it from the realm of the "historical." It served as a convenient stage on which Xenophon could produce his own didactic fairy tale, while disregarding the inconvenient realities of history.[21] Others assure us that Xenophon is merely following a well-established Greek tradition about Cyrus which can be seen in Aeschylus, Herodotus, Plato and Antisthenes.[22] These commentators may be right about the advantages offered by a chronologically and spatially distant setting and about the prior existence of a favorable Greek tradition about Cyrus. But they are wrong to imply that these considerations make Xenophon's choice less meaningful. He could have chosen, as he did in the *Hiero*, a setting from the Greek past, or, as Plato did in the *Republic*, a hypothetical situation. But he did not. He chose a Persian setting. I believe that, at

---

[20] They are "authentic" in the sense that these traditions were in circulation and were taken over by Xenophon. They were not necessarily all true representations of past events, any more than many of the traditions about early Greek history which surface in Herodotus' or Thucydides' pages. But no one has ever accused Herodotus of inventing the tale of Polycrates' ring.

[21] E.g. Breitenbach (above, note 14) 1708.

[22] E.g. Higgins (above, note 3) 44.

the very least, Xenophon should be credited with the capacity for making a deliberate and meaningful choice.

Several factors may help to account for Xenophon's choice of a Persian setting. In the first place, the situation begins to simplify itself if only one accepts Xenophon's own claims about the work. He said that he was exercised by the question — "How may one rule Mankind successfully?" If, in search of an answer to this question, he looked to Cyrus the Great and Old Persia, this ought not to occasion much surprise. Indeed, for an open-minded Greek of the fourth century it really should have been the obvious place to look. The greatness and capacity of Cyrus and the Persians as builders and rulers of a vast empire spoke for itself. Cyrus and his immediate successors had rapidly conquered an empire of unprecedented type and dimensions, encompassing a multitude of different peoples and extending (in modern geographical terms) from Turkey to India, from Russia to the Sudan. For almost two hundred years the Persian Empire had dominated most of the world as the Greeks knew it. For one who was in search of a solution to the problem of administering an empire, the authentic historical experience of Persia would clearly be of the utmost instructional value.

Any reasonable Greek might have reached this conclusion, but Xenophon had an advantage over most other reasonable Greeks — his own familiarity with the Persian Empire and its ruling people. To my mind, a large part of the inspiration for Xenophon's choice of a Persian setting is to be found in his contacts with the Persian prince Cyrus and other Persians in Cyrus' retinue during the march up-country to Babylonian Cunaxa in the year 401 B.C. These events, which he so eloquently described in the *Anabasis*, undoubtedly made a deep impression on the young Xenophon, and there are more than a few indications that he was captivated by the dashing young Persian prince with the famous name.

Many commentators have remarked upon the similarities between the younger Cyrus of the *Anabasis* and the elder Cyrus of the *Cyropaedia*.[23] Xenophon himself makes the connection in the encomium which he inserts after his account of the heroic death in battle of the prince at Cunaxa (*Anabasis* 1.9). The encomium opens with a suggestive evaluation of Cyrus:

---

[23] G. Cousin, *Kyros le jeune en Asie Mineure* (Nancy 1904) xli, has compiled a list of correspondences between the two Cyruses. The significance of these similarities is discussed below, pages 78-79.

He was a man who, of all the Persians who have lived since that ancient Cyrus, was both the most kingly and the most worthy to rule.

I wish to argue that the comparison was suggested to Xenophon by the younger Cyrus himself. When Cyrus set out to organize a rebellion against his brother, the Persian king Artaxerxes II, he must have known that he would need some sort of a propaganda theme which he could employ both to attract support for his cause and to justify his usurpation of the throne. It appears that he took advantage of his famous name and summoned up memories of a former period of greatness, the Old Persia of Cyrus the Great. Plutarch (*Artaxerxes* 6.3) preserves a remark of the younger Cyrus to the effect that Artaxerxes, because of his faintheartedness and softness, could neither keep his horse on the hunt nor his throne in a crisis. Cyrus may have argued that Artaxerxes was not worthy of the Persian throne. The famous Cyrus of the past had won an empire on account of his excellence, and the new Cyrus, who, as Xenophon says, was most like his namesake in kingliness and worthiness to rule, deserved to sit on the throne of empire and promised to revive the customs and qualities that had made Persia great.

Admittedly, this reconstruction of Cyrus' propaganda campaign is conjectural, but it can be confirmed by the counter-propaganda which issued from Artaxerxes' camp. If the rebel prince Cyrus was invoking the legendary Cyrus, it was to Artaxerxes' advantage to belittle this claim. One can detect this process at work in the *Persica* of Ctesias, a Greek who served as physician to Artaxerxes' family and lived at the Persian court at the time of the younger Cyrus' rebellion. Whereas Herodotus and Xenophon agree that the elder Cyrus was the son of Cambyses, Ctesias makes him a commoner, son of a low-born cutthroat named Atradates and his goatherd wife Argoste, who began his career as a servant at the Median court.[24] This is tantamount to a denial that Cyrus was an Achaemenid, a member of the legitimate line of Persian kings.

Cyrus was also removed from the official genealogy of the royal family. A pair of Old Persian inscriptions on gold tablets which were found at Ecbatana carry the names of Ariaramnes and Arsames, addressing each as "the great King, King of Kings, King in Persia."[25]

---

[24] Felix Jacoby, *Die Fragmente der griechischen Historiker* II.1 (Berlin 1926), no. 90 F 66.

[25] These inscriptions are found in R.G. Kent, *Old Persian*, 2nd. ed. (New Haven 1953). They are listed as AmH and AsH on page 116.

Ariaramnes and Arsames were the great-grandfather and grandfather of Darius I, a member of a junior branch of the Achaemenid clan, who wrested power from the line of Cyrus in the 520s. These two shadowy figures had not been kings of Persia,[26] and the terminology used in these inscriptions — "King of Kings" — is wrong for the period of vassalage to Media. Orientalists feel that the orthography of these inscriptions is appropriate to the time of Artaxerxes II, and Kent has suggested that they may have been part of an anti-Cyrus propaganda campaign related to the revolt of Cyrus the younger.[27] By erecting these inscriptions, Artaxerxes is claiming that the legitimate royal line is that of Darius. Cyrus the founder is being ousted from the royal line, and in this way Artaxerxes hopes to counter his brother's pretensions to revive the Old Persia of Cyrus the Great.[28]

[26] It is known from Darius I's monumental inscription at Behistun that Ariaramnes and Arsames were his great-grandfather and grandfather in the line of Achaemenes, the eponymous ancestor (Kent [above, note 25] DB 1.3-6, pp. 116, 119). Darius does not specifically claim that these immediate ancestors were kings, though he may have hoped that the reader would draw this conclusion, since he then claims, with studied ambiguity, that eight members of his "family" (*taumā*) had been kings before him (DB 1.8-11). At any rate, they could not have been, since the Cyrus Cylinder tells us that Cyrus' royal predecessors and ancestors were Cambyses, Cyrus and Teispes (translated in James B. Pritchard, ed., *Ancient Near Eastern Texts Relating to the Old Testament*, 2nd ed. [Princeton 1955] 315-16).

[27] Kent (above, note 25) 12.

[28] There is an intriguing postscript to this war of propaganda waged between the camps of Cyrus and Artaxerxes over the reputation of a long-dead ancestor. Iranian archaeologists have recently been devoting attention to a tomb at Buzpar, in southwest Fars province, which appears to be a humbler replica of the tomb of Cyrus the Great at Pasargadae. It has been proposed that this may be the tomb of the younger Cyrus, put there by the queen mother, Parysatis, who, according to our sources, had always favored the younger son. If this be the case, one should not miss the meaning of her choice of model. Achaemenid kings and members of the royal family had, since the days of Darius, abandoned the free-standing pedestal-type tomb, such as was constructed for Cyrus at Pasargadae, and preferred instead monumental tombs carved out of cliff faces, such as those at Naqsh-i Rustam near Persepolis. If Parysatis, or whoever saw to the burial of the younger Cyrus, returned to the old tomb-type, it should be regarded as a conspicuous continuation of the identification between the younger and elder Cyrus upon which the young prince had tried to capitalize. For the posited tomb of the younger Cyrus see A. Shahbazi, "The Achaemenid Tomb in Buzpar (Gur-i Dukhtar)," *Bastan Chenassi va Honar-e Iran* 9/10 (1972) 56; Boyce (above, note 4) 210.

However, David Stronach, in a personal communication, has expressed his doubts about the identification of the Buzpar tomb as that of the younger Cyrus. He points out that it is too modest for a member of the royal family, that the Tomb of Cyrus was visible for anyone to see and copy, and that there were no cliffs available in

Xenophon will have been exposed to the propaganda of the younger Cyrus while he was traveling with the prince, for this propaganda was directed primarily at the Persians in Cyrus' camp.[29] It thus appears that the comparison of the two Cyruses was an idea which

the remote Buzpar valley. He prefers to see it as the tomb of some local dynast. For the tomb of Cyrus the Great, see below, note 37.

[29] It is legitimate to ask how Xenophon would have communicated with Persians in Cyrus' camp and whether he would have had much personal contact with Cyrus himself. As for the first, a language barrier certainly existed, but it will not have been insurmountable. There is no reason to think that Xenophon knew Persian or any other Near Eastern language. But the record of similar situations in antiquity and in our own day teaches us that people thrown together in a situation like that of the multi-ethnic army traveling with Cyrus usually manage to communicate. Of course sign language, gestures and pictures can only be used to communicate messages of the most basic sort. But there were no doubt many non-Greeks who learned some Greek, and some Greeks learned enough Aramaic, the *lingua franca* of the Persian Empire, to converse with their Near Eastern counterparts. Thus, I see no obstacle to Xenophon collecting information from barbarian songs and stories, as he tells us he did, even if at second or third hand and in translation. Herodotus, who, so far as can be told, spoke no foreign languages, had done so before him.

As to whether Xenophon was on familiar terms with Cyrus, it is not easy to say. He had been formally presented to Cyrus by his friend and host Proxenus (*Anabasis* 3.1.8), and it would appear from their chance encounter just before the clash at Cunaxa that Cyrus knew Xenophon by sight (*Anabasis* 1.8.15-17). Cyrus certainly spoke Greek, as demonstrated by his brief conversation with Xenophon just before the battle and by several incidents on the march to Babylonia (e.g. 1.5.15-17, where Cyrus addresses two quarreling factions of Greek soldiers). But Xenophon was technically a mere observer and probably had not participated in the council meetings which Cyrus held with his commanders. Thus, there is no direct evidence that Xenophon and Cyrus had spent any significant amount of time together.

On the other hand, I see no reason why they should not have been acquainted. After all, Xenophon had come along on the expedition in order to win the favor and seek the patronage of Cyrus (*Anabasis* 3.1.4-5). Cyrus was always interested in cultivating Greeks who could be useful to him and Xenophon was a member of that class of Greek aristocrats to which belonged a number of Cyrus' mercenary commanders. Furthermore, it is hard to account for Xenophon's assumption of a leadership role with the Ten Thousand after the death of Cyrus if he had not been a figure of some prominence earlier. Finally, Xenophon's obvious infatuation with Cyrus must have been sparked by some personal contact, even if it is conceded that he was young and easily impressed.

However, even if it cannot be demonstrated that Xenophon had spent time with Cyrus, this still does not mean that he could not have been exposed to Cyrus' program of propaganda. He could have picked this up from his friend Proxenus and the other Greek commanders, who were in contact with Cyrus, or from other soldiers or civilians in Cyrus' camp. No doubt the camp was always abuzz with stories of Cyrus. What else did Xenophon have to do on the march to Babylonia?

Xenophon derived from his Persian patron. But he took over more than this. The package of propaganda being disseminated by the rebel prince presumably incorporated a picture of Cyrus the founder which the new Cyrus undertook to emulate and a concept of Old Persia which he promised to restore. I would therefore go so far as to say that Xenophon received a very particular vision of Cyrus the Great and Old Persia from the younger Cyrus himself.

So powerful was the impression which this made on Xenophon that he could not easily disassociate the younger Cyrus from the ancestor whom he claimed to imitate and, in a sense, reincarnate.[30] There are a fair number of passages in the *Cyropaedia* in which Xenophon remarks upon a trait or habit of the elder Cyrus in terms similar or identical to those used for the younger Cyrus in the *Anabasis*. They undergo comparable educations, show a remarkable aptitude and enthusiasm for its basic features—riding, shooting, hunting—and excel over all other boys in their age-group. Each is susceptible, as a youth, to reckless daring. Each has the habit of exercising before meals, each sends food to friends as a gesture of affection, and each proclaims his desire to outdo friends and enemies at doing good and harm respectively. Finally, there are multiple correspondences, sometimes in virtually identical phraseology, between Xenophon's description of the younger Cyrus' conduct as satrap in Asia Minor and his account of the elder Cyrus' efforts to guarantee the security of his person by winning popularity among friends, potential rivals and subjects.[31] It is hard to resist the conclusion that, insofar as Xenophon paints a portrait of the character, conduct and personal relations of the elder Cyrus, it is based largely on the personality of his one-time patron, Cyrus the prince.

If, as has been maintained here, Xenophon modeled the figure of Cyrus the Great on the personality of the younger Cyrus, and he derived a vision of Old Persia in the time of the founder from the hopes, dreams and self-serving claims of the younger Cyrus, this does not constitute grounds for accusing Xenophon of lack of concern for

---

[30] Xenophon also makes the connection between the two in a problematic passage in the *Oeconomicus* (4.16-19), where he seems to slide almost unconsciously from the elder to the younger Cyrus, without making the reader aware of the transition.
[31] Education—*Cyr.* 1.2.2-1.3.1; 1.4.5. *Anab.* 1.9.2-6. Daring—*Cyr.* 1.4.8; 1.4.21. *Anab.* 1.9.6; 1.8.24-27. Exercise—*Cyr.* 8.1.37. *Oeconomicus* 4.29. Gifts of Food—*Cyr.* 8.2.3; 8.4.6. *Anab.* 1.9.25-26. Doing Good and Harm—*Cyr.* 5.3.32. *Anab.* 1.9.11. Administration—*Cyr.* 8.2. *Anab.* 1.9.7-31.

historical accuracy or willful distortion of truth. The personality of Cyrus, dead now for one hundred and fifty years and encrusted with layer upon layer of legend, was irrecoverable. Where was Xenophon to turn for an accurate picture of conditions in sixth century Iran? Thucydides (1.1.3) had complained of the insurmountable difficulties facing one who tried to reconstruct the history of the remote past and he was not even thinking about the additional barriers which had to be faced in dealing with an alien culture. Xenophon worked with what he had. The fullest and most vivid picture of Cyrus and Old Persia available to him came from the camp of the younger Cyrus. To the extent that the *Cyropaedia* violates history, this is at least partially due, not to bald invention on Xenophon's part, but to the fact that he had to rely on his sources, written and oral, with the younger Cyrus prominent among the latter.

How historically reliable is the *Cyropaedia*? The *communis opinio*, as has been seen, holds that Xenophon indulged in free invention of allegedly historical events. Critics are especially quick to pounce whenever Xenophon contradicts the "historical" tradition found in Herodotus. Yet there are occasions when it can be confirmed from Oriental evidence that Xenophon is correct where Herodotus is wrong or lacks information. A case in point involves the ancestry of Cyrus. Herodotus had accepted the folklore motif of Cyrus' exposure as a baby and made his father Cambyses "well born and of a quiet temper... much lower than a Mede of middle estate" (1.107). Xenophon, on the other hand, correctly reports that Cyrus was the son of Cambyses, King of Persia, a principality within the Median Empire (*Cyropaedia* 1.2.1). This is confirmed by the so-called Cyrus Cylinder, a propaganda tract in Akkadian cuneiform composed after the capture of Babylon, presumably at the behest of Cyrus, which gives his lineage as:

> ...son of Cambyses, great king, king of Anshan... of a family which always (exercised) kingship...[32]

As Xenophon's Cyrus is poised to attack Assyria (by which name Xenophon refers to the neo-Babylonian kingdom),[33] he gains the

---

[32] The Cyrus Cylinder is translated in Pritchard (above, note 26) 315-316.
[33] See Peyton R. Helm, *"Greeks" in the Neo-Assyrian Levant and "Assyria" in Early Greek Writers* (dissertation University of Pennsylvania 1980).

allegiance of the Assyrian vassal Gobryas, who later plays an important part in the capture of Babylon (*Cyropaedia* 4.6.1; 7.5.24-30). This time confirmation comes from the Nabonidus Chronicle, a contemporary cuneiform document which describes, among other events of the reigns of Nabonidus and Cyrus, the fall of Babylon. One Ugbaru, the Babylonian governor of Gutium, accompanied Cyrus when he took Babylon and helped with the initial administrative reorganization.[34] Nothing of this individual and his role is known to Herodotus.

Such examples provide a salutary warning that it is rash to see Xenophon as invariably mistaken or guilty of a fabrication whenever he disagrees with Herodotus or reports an incident or detail which has not chanced to be confirmed elsewhere. Let me emphasize this point with a final substantial example.

Xenophon's account of the death of Cyrus is regularly cited as a blatant example of the liberties which Xenophon takes with the established "history" of Cyrus. It is assumed that he simply invented his version because it suited his literary and didactic purposes, that is, the glorification and idealization of Cyrus, although he knew the truth full well from reading Herodotus.

In Herodotus' pages Cyrus dies a sudden and violent death in battle against the Massagetae. His body is captured, and the bloodthirsty nomad queen sticks his head in a sack of blood and taunts him. All too often it is forgotten that Herodotus goes on to say:

> Many stories are related of Cyrus' death; this, that I have told, is the worthiest of credence. (1.214)

A very different account is found in the waning pages of the *Cyropaedia* (8.7). Cyrus, now far advanced in years, has returned to the Persian homeland. A dream informs him that he is soon to die, and shortly thereafter he becomes weak and bedridden. Summoning his sons, his friends and the Persian officials, he proclaims his last will and testament. Cambyses, the elder son, is to be king, while Tanaoxares is to receive the satrapies of Media, Armenia and Cadusia. Both are urged to love each other and to treat all men fairly. Cyrus also gives instructions for his burial.

Much of the content of Cyrus' deathbed oration is invented by Xenophon. Cyrus' declaration that he has always avoided *hubris*, knowing that misfortune could strike at any time and that no man can be

---

[34] The Nabonidus Chronicle is translated in Pritchard (above, note 26) 306-307.

accounted truly blessed until he is dead, is a thoroughly Greek sentiment which immediately calls to mind the lecture of Solon to Croesus
in Herodotus' pages. Cyrus' discourse on the immortality of the soul
is reminiscent of the speeches of Socrates as he prepares to die in Plato's
Apology and *Phaedo*.

However, the historical framework of the scene is manifestly not
the invention of Xenophon. For there is a strikingly similar account
of the last moments of Cyrus in the earlier *Persica* of Ctesias.[35] Here
Cyrus is wounded in battle against the Derbici, an obscure central
Asian people. He is carried back to his camp, where he lingers for
several days. Before dying he must have summoned his friends and
family, for he appoints Cambyses to succeed him as king, while making
the younger son, Tanyoxarkes, master of Bactria, Choramnia, Par-
thia and Carmania. He urges his friends and family to show love for
one another, praying for blessings on those who abide in mutual good
fellowship and cursing those who initiate evil.

One can readily discern that Xenophon has drawn upon either
Ctesias or the tradition from which Ctesias derived. Both have a
deathbed scene in which the moribund monarch summons his family and associates in order to deliver his last will and testament. In
both versions the younger son is called Tanaoxares/Tanyoxarkes,
whereas he is known in our other sources by some variant of Persian
Bardiya, [36] and he is given a command comprising several regions
in central Asia. In both versions Cyrus urges concord upon those who
survive him, and he dies in the presence of family and friends. If the
full text of Ctesias' account of this event had survived, rather than
Photius' brief epitome, it might be possible to point to even more
correspondences.

Any consideration of which version is to be preferred must take
into account an additional factor—the tomb of Cyrus. In Xenophon's
dramatic deathbed scene, Cyrus discusses arrangements for his own
burial. It is known that Cyrus was buried in a stately tomb at
Pasargadae.[37] This tomb was visited and restored by Alexander the

---

[35] Felix Jacoby, *Die Fragmente der griechischen Historiker* IIIC (Leiden 1958), no. 688
F 9.

[36] Bardiya in the Behistun inscription, Marphius in Hellanicus (ap. Schol. Aeschylus
Persae 775), Mardos in Aeschylus *Persae* 774, Smerdis in Herodotus, Mergis or Mer-
dis in Justin.

[37] For the tomb of Cyrus see David Stronach, *Pasargadae, A Report on the Excavations
Conducted by the British Institute of Persian Studies from 1961 to 1963* (Oxford 1978) 24-43.

Great, and is described by the historians of that era. From their reports
one can be certain that it was no cenotaph, but rather housed the
body of Cyrus.[38] This fact can easily be accounted for by the versions of the death of Cyrus given by Xenophon and Ctesias, for
Xenophon has him expire in Persia and Ctesias maintains that Cambyses had the body of Cyrus returned from the land of the Derbici
to Persia, where it was buried.[39] But it is hard to reconcile the tomb
of Cyrus at Pasargadae with Herodotus' account, in which Cyrus' body
is captured and dismembered by the vengeful Massagetae.

Finally, as Christensen has shown, Xenophon's overall conception
of the death of Cyrus is firmly rooted in Iranian tradition.[40] In the
Shahnama of Ferdowsi, which preserves the cultural concepts and story
patterns of ancient Iranian oral tradition, the life of the ideal king
ends with a scene in which the dying king summons family, friends
and advisers, arranges the succession, makes known his last wishes,
and communicates to his successors a political testament. The conclusion of the *Cyropaedia* fits precisely into this mold.

It must be emphasized that no attempt is being made here to argue
for the historicity of the *Cyropaedia* as a whole. Numerous episodes,
conversations, speeches and private encounters must have been invented by Xenophon, for there could have been no possible source
for such material. And it is precisely in these scenes, the didactic and
philosophical core of the *Cyropaedia*, that the patently Greek elements
of thought, speech and values are strongest. However, it should now
be acknowledged that this core is set into a historical and cultural
framework, and that, for the construction of this framework,
Xenophon had access to credible sources — Greek written sources,
Greek and barbarian oral tradition, and the example of Persian
customs and institutions of his own day. As a result, the *Cyropaedia*
contains a greater quantity of valuable information about Persian
history, culture and institutions than is generally recognized, and even
where one is inclined to doubt the historicity of a given event, it should
be conceded that Xenophon may have preserved an authentic Greek
or barbarian tradition — however false or distorted — about Persian

[38] Aristobulus ap. Arrian *Anabasis* 6.29, Strabo 15.3.7. Aristobulus ought to have
known, for he was appointed by Alexander to restore the tomb of Cyrus. See Robin
Lane Fox, *Alexander the Great* (London and New York 1973) 408, 542.

[39] Jacoby (above, note 35), no. 688 F 13.

[40] Christensen (above, note 8) 122-35.

history. The student of ancient Iran would be foolish to neglect the *Cyropaedia* or reject it out of hand.

I have argued above that Xenophon received a particularly vivid picture of Cyrus the Great and Old Persia from the entourage of the younger Cyrus. Obviously this vision of the Persian past is not likely to be correct in all essentials. After all, not only was it part of a campaign of political propaganda meant to justify Cyrus' ambition, but there is no reason to believe that there existed, in ancient Iran, a critical historical tradition which would have made possible an accurate recreation of the events, personalities and conditions of the sixth century. But the traditions embodied in the *Cyropaedia* may, in some degree, represent a different sort of truth. It may reflect the Persians' own conceptions about their past, and would thereby provide us with precious insights into the traditions and values of the aristocracy in fourth century Persia. As such, it would be analogous to the early books of Livy, which, if they preserve little that is historically accurate about Rome in the era of the Kings and the earliert days of the Republic, do constitute a priceless treasury of conceptions about the past held by Romans in the late Republic and early Empire.

One last consideration is in order. How did Xenophon conceive of his achievement in writing the *Cyropaedia*? We in the modern world tend to treat the boundary between truth and fiction as absolute, as clearly separating two different and irreconcilable orders of things. But it is, I suppose, now widely recognized that this boundary was a shifting and permeable one for the people of classical antiquity.[41] Of course, any formulation of Xenophon's own conception of his mission must inevitably remain tentative, but I suspect that his situation might profitably be compared to that of a pair of modern writers who are usually classified as authors of "historical fiction." Robert Graves and Gore Vidal have both written stories set in the ancient world, and both have, on occasion, issued revealing protests against the classification of their works as "fiction."[42] Each insists in his own way

---

[41] See, most recently, the valuable observations of T.P. Wiseman, *Clio's Cosmetics: Three Studies in Greco-Roman Literature* (Leicester 1979); Emilio Gabba, "True History and False History in Classical Antiquity," *Journal of Roman Studies* 71 (1981) 50-62.

[42] Robert Graves, Preface to *Claudius the God* (New York 1935) 5-6: "Few incidents here given are wholly unsupported by historical authority of some sort or other and I hope none are historically incredible." Gore Vidal, Afterword to *Burr* (New York 1973) 429-30: "...the story told is history and not invention."

that, though he is not a professional historian, his work is based on historical research and represents a reconstruction of the past. If it be permitted to recast their claims in Aristotle's terms, the implication is that their works are valuable, not only for the general truths about human affairs which fiction seeks to convey, but also for the particular truths which derive from knowledge of the actual events and conditions of the past.

Xenophon probably lacked the self-awareness of these modern writers, and the relevant categories of history and novel were only in process of formation in his time. But I wonder whether he would not have seen himself in a similar light, and have claimed that the *Cyropaedia* offered both particular truths to be garnered from the record of the past and the higher truths which he superimposed by artistic license.[43, 44]

---

[43] In this connection it is interesting to note that many readers in antiquity regarded the *Cyropaedia* as an historical work. This is true of Plato (*Laws* III.694C ff.), Dionysius of Halicarnassus (Letter to Pompeius Geminus 4.777) and those Hellenistic historians who modeled their lives of Alexander and other leading figures of the age on the *Cyropaedia*. The denial of Cicero (*Epist. ad* Q. *Fr.* 1.1.23) that Xenophon intended to write history in the *Cyropaedia* carries the clear implication that some people felt otherwise. These passages are briefly summarized and analyzed by Farber (above, note 3) vi-xiv.

[44] I would like to express my appreciation to Professors A.E. Raubitschek and M.H. Jameson for their overall support and invaluable contributions to my research on Xenophon. I also owe a large debt of gratitude to Professor J.K. Anderson, who offered perceptive criticisms of earlier written and oral versions of this paper, and to Professor J.W. Zarker, who reviewed the final draft. Obviously the responsibility for the finished product is my own.

Limit, Propriety, and Transgression in the Histories of Herodotus

DONALD LATEINER

Ohio Wesleyan University

I

The personality of a writer can be found only in his text. There we may detect patterns of thought, habitual standards of comparison, concepts of relevance and significance, historiographical notions, and ideas about morality and causality.

Herodotus' report on distant places and by-gone times attempted to overcome his contemporaries' conceptual limitations. However, the elucidation of Herodotus' own ideas and attitudes has been hindered by the bulk of his *Histories* and their perplexing structure. His literary invention, the *Histories*, exhibits the usual problems of experimental literature, including consistency, intelligibility and coherence. For instance, although Herodotus has characteristic ideas, expressions, and linguistic habits, his work lacks a dominant theory, a regulating ideology, or a controlling metaphor that can aid, or indeed, hinder historical understanding and research, and win a following. Only recently have we emerged from the shadow of the metaphoric notion of "decline and fall" for the Roman Empire. Historians now happily speak of "organic transformation" and even a "salutary dislocation."[1]

---

[1] P. Brown, *The World of Late Antiquity* (London 1971) 38. On Gibbon's "controlling metaphor," see L. Braudy, *Narrative Form in History and Fiction* (Princeton 1970) 215-16. "Periodization" can have the same distorting and beneficial consequences.

"Manifest Destiny" and similar catchwords produce national policy and works of history. The image of the state as a living organism, the "body politic," perhaps an animal (e.g., Hobbes) or a man-shaped monster, can derail discourse in politics and history. Aristotle described Attic tragedy as experiencing a biological evolution that reached maturity. Polybius mechanically posited a necessary old age and decay to the "natural growth" of the Roman state.[2] Ancient authors do not comment on the hidden authority of these literary devices.

While Herodotus has no governing image or idea that articulates or controls his entire work, several clusters of concepts frequently recur: one concerns boundaries and proper limits. This loose set of ideas helps to define the effective forces in the *Histories*.

Today I examine three facets of the concept of limit in Herodotus' text: the *metaphors* of proper bounds and transgression; the intrusion of an "off-limits" *subject*, women, into the mostly male realm of war and government, where they provide a contrast to the usual historical actions and a relevant horizon of "normality;" and the frequent illustration of two related *moral principles*, "mind your own business" and "pay your debts," adages of propriety whose neglect leads to the extermination of families and nations.

II

Herodotus has no over-arching or controlling image or metaphor that submits his narrative to a known pattern. The recurrent image and metaphor, however, of the proper realm and its limits, the transgression of which leads to failure, has resonant analogues throughout the work. This conceptual nexus of boundary and transgression can be found in earlier literature, for instance in the Presocratic philosophers (e.g., Anaximander F1; Heraclitus F94, 120; Parmenides F8), Aeschylus' *Persians*, and the Persian War epigrams.

There are delimited spheres in every realm. One can discover territorial limit in the animal kingdom for lions, adders, birds, ants, etc. The Egyptian ibis keeps out Arabian flying snakes (2.75. 3; also 5.10 and 7.126). Vegetable species such as myrrh, cinnamon, and frankincense have their own habitats (3.106-107). Anything that exceeds limit, or has an unusual nature, constitutes a *thoma* and deserves

---

[2] *Poetics* 4 = 1449A14-15; Polybius 6.9.10-14; cf. K. von Fritz, *Aristotle's Contribution to the Practice and Theory of Historiography* (Howison Lecture, 1957), *U. Cal. Publ. in Philosophy* 28/3 (Berkeley and Los Angeles 1958) 128.

description, such as the camel's amusing peculiarities (3.109).[3] Similarly, in the human realm, a man must remain within his proper nature and territory, look to his own family and property. Similarly, land masses must not be confused. The Persians are reported to believe, at the beginning of the *History*, that Asia is the property of the Persians, Europe of the Greeks (1.4.4); near the end of his work, in counterpoise, Herodotus mentions once more Persia's claim to Asia, separate from the Greeks (9.116.3). The tale of Xerxes' attempt to bring together the two separate realms is concluded—it is the last recorded historical event in the book—with the Greek dedication of the broken cables that once briefly and disastrously linked Europe and Asia (9.121).[4] Europe and Asia were intended to be separate, one is meant to understand, a truth central also to Aeschylus' *Persai*.

Herodotus has oracular testimony to argue against interfering with nature, making land into sea (1.174.3-6). The Pythia declared that "Zeus would have made [Cnidus] an island, if he so desired." Thus, when one reads of preparations for Xerxes' Athos canal, or, *a fortiori* for Xerxes' Hellespont bridge, the attentive know that these efforts will have unhappy consequences (7.22.1, etc.; 7.34-36). Xerxes had the delimiting waters whipped because they demolished his first bridge. "Rivers... are boundaries not only in the geographic sense,"[5] but they also have a moral significance. They present a choice, a point of no return, and "The crossing of rivers... is always used to prove the *hybris* of the aggressor."[6] The Halys was Croesus' limit, the Danube Darius' (4.142). Xerxes' moral transgression is compounded, since the historian reports that the Persians, more than any other people, worshipped rivers (1.138.2).

Every "realm" is defined by "boundary," οὖρος. Sometimes the boundary is one of nature's laws, as the limit to a man's life (1.32.2*

---

[3] See H. Barth, "Zur Bewertung und Auswahl des Stoffes durch Herodot," *Klio* 50 (1968) 93-110.

[4] H. Immerwahr, "Aspects of Historical Causation in Herodotus," *TAPA* 85 (1956) 250; idem, *Form and Thought in Herodotus* (Cleveland 1966) 43.

[5] Fr. Solmsen, "Two Crucial Decisions in Herodotus," *Mededelingen... Nederl. Akad.* 37/6 (1974) 5, note 10, referring to Immerwahr (above, note 4: 1966) 84, note 17, and 293, who refers to R. von Scheliha, *Die Wassergrenzung im Altertum* (diss. Breslau 1931). See p. 11 of von Scheliha's monograph.

[6] Immerwahr (above, note 4: 1966) 293. This is excessively schematic. See, e.g., 1.191; 2.124.2; 5.11.1; 5.23.1; 8.25.1 (the last four are straits rather than rivers); 5.52.2, 77.2, 83.1; 6.2.2, 5.2, 70.2 (*bis*); 9.6 (*bis*), etc.

[an asterisk marks every reference to passages in direct speech], 216.2), or the range and territory of European lions (7.126), or an eclipse (1.74.3). More often, Herodotus' "boundaries" are the product of political geography, sometimes natural features that serve as political divisions, such as the Halys river dividing the Persian from the Lydian empire, or the Euphrates dividing Cilicia from Armenia (1.72.2; 5.52.3). One hears of the boundaries of Egypt, of the Agathyrsi, of the Calyndians (2.17.1-2; 4.125.4; 1.172.2; etc.). The first chapter of the *Histories* assumes an anachronistic Hellenic-Asiatic enmity and division, and the last, epilogic chapter distinguishes a proper realm for hardy, free Persians that is different from the fertile realms of docile slaves. Both framing chapters, whatever other meanings they carry, deal with the problem of natural and proper bounds.

Everything in the human realm has its limits, nothing is boundless, ἄπειρον, except, hyperbolically, the lands beyond the Danube and the Plain of the Caucasus (5.91; 1.204.1). An oracle from Ammon decides a dispute over the boundaries of Egypt (2.18.2-3), suggesting that limits are a divine concern, dangerous for man to meddle with. Distance itself has significance, political and monitory.

The Persians, Herodotus reports, hypostatize distance into a *political* value. They themselves rule the nations closest to them and allow these neighboring subjects to rule those *more distant*. This is only to be expected of a people that "honors and respects — after themselves — those who dwell nearest them, honor thirdly the next farthest and thereafter in order of proximity" (3.89.1; 1.134.2).

Herodotus employs various forms of ἕκας, "far," to mark the concept of a liminal area, when men dangerously stray beyond their own territory. The Asiatic Ethiopians live *further* from Persia than the eastern Indians and do not recognize Persian suzerainty (3.101.2). The Spartans tell the Plataeans that they live *too far* from them to offer active alliance; they advise them to approach their neighbors, the Athenians (6.108.2*). Themistocles tells Eurybiades that if the Greeks fight and conquer at Salamis, the Persians will get no *further* (8.60γ*).

Artabanus advises Xerxes: "The land [of Greece] itself will be your enemy. If nothing stands up to you, the *farther* you get, the more opposed to you distance becomes. You will always be cheated by what lies just beyond... The more land you cover and the more time you spend there, the more you will starve" (7.49. 4-5*; cf. Aesch. *Pers.* 792). This resembles Cyrus' rebuke of Artembares' desire for *Lebensraum* in the epilogue. Cambyses foolishly sets out with his army "for

the ends of the earth" (3.25.1, ἔσχατα γῆς) without supplies. He cannot calculate limits to his power, megalomaniac that he is. Herodotus
solemnly commemorates the *furthest* points west that Aryandes' army
invading Libya and Mardonius' army in Europe reached (4.204; 9.14).
The formulaic phrases celebrate the accomplishment but also mark
the imposed necessity of turning back. The nearly identical and formulaic statements in these instances record a limit that ought not to
become forgotten, one of the Proem's principles of relevance.

Limits ought not to be transgressed, but they are, and their transgression functions as a cause, necessary and sometimes sufficient, of
historically significant events. Xerxes' crossing of the Hellespont (esp.
7.34-36, 53.2-57.1) presents the most fully articulated and best-known
example of human transgression in the *Histories*, in which moral and
physical transgression run parallel.[7] Darius at the Ister offers an earlier
example, where water again marks the dangerous liminal act (4.118.1).
At Plataea, the crossing of the Asopus constitutes another symbolic
transgression. The Greeks are told by their seer that they will conquer if they remain in place, but they will lose the battle if they cross
the stream (9.36). Mardonius obtained the same message from heaven,
so for two days neither side crossed (37.1, 40). Mardonius finally led
his troops across the Asopus and, as predicted, lost the battle (59.1).
The *Histories* are pulled together by this correspondence of events on
very different levels and scales that should guide one's reading of a
seemingly amorphous text.

Herodotus sees moral transgression on both sides. The Greeks share
responsibility in both the mythical (1.1-5) and the historical version,
where Herodotus speaks of the war which the Greeks and Persians
"began to fight against each other" (Proem). And although Croesus
began the series of injustices, the Greeks get blamed for bringing the
Persian Wars on themselves (1.5.3; 5.97.3). The often sinister verb
of "crossing," διαβαίνειν, appears last (9.114.2) when the Greeks sail
north to Abydus. From there the Spartans return home while the Athenians "cross over" to Sestus and besiege it. Now they commence a
series of aggressive acts. Sestus, to be sure, is in Europe, but the *crossing*
marks the radical change from a Hellenic *defensive* to an Athenian *offensive* campaign, a moment not meaningless to an audience in 430 B.C.
From Darius, who first "planned to bridge (ζεύξας) this continent here
[Asia] to the other one, for the conquest of Scythia" (3.134.4*), to

---

[7] See Immerwahr (above, note 4: 1966) 84, 293; also Aesch. *Pers.* 65.

Xerxes who did it again, the Persians try to "render Persian territory coterminous with Zeus' heaven" (7.8γ 1*).[8] They failed, Herodotus believed, in part because their attempt disregarded proper realms and boundaries.

Herodotus' use of the concept of bound and transgression implies a moral criticism of aggressive war and imperialism. Herodotus sees war as a calamity. The Athenian and Eretrian ships dispatched to Ionia are described Homerically as the "beginning of evils for both Greeks and barbarians." The Delian earthquake signified the commencement of three generations of war with more calamities than the previous twenty (approximately seven hundred years) had witnessed. When Herodotus praises the Athenians for yielding hegemony of the Greek forces before Salamis, he asserts that "discord within a nation is as much worse than war fought with a united front, as war itself is worse than peace."[9] To be sure, a defensive war can be justifiable and necessary. This was true of the Panhellenic alliance against the Persian invasion.

The Athenians, he implies, perceived proper boundaries in their policies, at least until after the battle of Mycale. The Spartans at first drew too narrow a limit to Greece at the Isthmus, but then cooperated in defending not merely their land or their league, but all mainland Greece. Hellenic perception of *proper limits*, and the justified defense of *their own families* and land, promoted the successful repulse of Persian aggression.

Herodotus' reasoning may sometimes appear metaphysical, but he supplies historical causes sufficient to explain the historical failures.[10] The metaphoric complex of limit and transgression, at once biological, strategic, political, and moral, never exhausts his attempt to understand major events, but suggests certain underlying principles of action in man and nature. Herodotus offers *apodexis*, *memoranda* and *comparanda*, not abstract explanation or instruction. One is often shown and affected rather than taught.[11] Events that reflect on each other

---

[8] Cf. G. Cameron, "Ancient Persia," in *The Idea of History in the Ancient Near East*, ed. R.C. Denton (New Haven 1955; reprinted 1967), 83 quoting the Cyrus-cylinder (v. 22) on which Cyrus is "king of totality, great king, mighty king... king of the four world quarters."

[9] 5.97.3; 1.87.4*; 6.98.2; 7.104.3*; 8.3.1. Cf. Pindar's equally disapproving attitude towards war: frg.99 (Bowra).

[10] Ch. Hignett, *Xerxes' Invasion of Greece* (Oxford 1963) 36.

[11] J. Redfield, *Nature and Culture in the Iliad* (Chicago 1975) 43, on Homer.

by verbal and structural "coincidences" help explain each other to the reader, not by offering an explanation of why they happened, but by suggesting appropriate historical comparisons. We turn next to a subject that oscillates between history and fictions, private and public: women in fifth-century historiography.

III

> But history, real solemn history... the quarrels of... kings, with wars and pestilences, in every page... and hardly any women at all—it is very tiresome... (Jane Austen, *Northanger Abbey*, Ch. xiv)

Women, symbolic of the family, the household, the private realm that generally plays little part in Western historiography, have a special function in the *Histories* of the first historian. Women are mentioned in Herodotus with unusual frequency by most historians' standards, occasionally because they were ruling queens, tyrants, or monarchs' wives, [12] but generally because of their ordinary role in family and social life, their normative function. There is no separate and systematic study of females,[13] but, particularly in exotic climes, any habit by which they upset typical Greek social practice receives mention. That is to say, women are prior to, and outside, the realm of politics and provide certain glimpses of a given culture that the typical historian ignores. Herodotus combines anthropology with history.

Most of the references to women, as individuals or as a class, are in the earlier books, especially I, II, and IV, where anthropological curiosity is at its acme. Herodotus subscribes to conventional Greek

---

[12] Nitocris of Babylon (1.185.1), Tomyris of the Massagetae (1.205.1), and Artemisia of Halicarnassus (7.99.1, 3) are all admired for cleverness and judgment, the last even for her ἀνδρηίη, "manly courage," a marvelous paradox to Herodotus. Tomyris even shares Herodotus' enthusiasm for arbitration. Pheretime of Cyrene (4.165.1), Nitocris of Egypt (2.100.2-3), and the queens of Persia are, however, notable chiefly for their monstrous deeds.

[13] See, e.g., Elise Boulding, *The Underside of History* (Boulder, Colorado 1976). For antiquity, Sarah Pomeroy, *Goddesses, Whores, Wives, and Slaves* (New York 1975); or *Histoire mondiale de la femme*, ed. P. Grimal, I (Paris 1965), 4 vols. (1965-66). On women in Herodotus, Simon Pembroke, "Women in Charge," *JWCI* 30 (1967) 1-35, offers some anthropological observations, and some correction of Herodotus' ideas. For a thorough survey, see Carolyn Dewald, "Women and Culture in Herodotus' *Histories*," *Women's Studies* 8 (1981) 93-127.

male attitudes towards women; that they should be submissive and remain secluded. Generally, women are merely sexual objects, either bluntly equated with property, or considered to be necessary machines for producing children, or reported as helpless victims of men's lust.[14] Euelthon of Salamis well expresses the conventional, condescending attitude towards women when he grants ferocious Pheretime not the army that she wants but a golden spindle, a distaff, and some wool (4.162.5). A woman says that Darius should prove himself to be a man, the only sex fit to rule Persians (3.134.2*). Oriental women, other than royalty, are sometimes portrayed with an exaggerated meanness of status. Their supposed subjection again points a contrast to Greek "respect" for women. Herodotus does not dissemble his Hellenic bias in issues relating to women. Certain activities are presented as not suitable for women, or at least not acceptable by Greek standards. Female chariot-drivers among the Zaueces (4.193), Egyptian women parading with ithyphallic puppets (2.48.2), and particularly savage acts of violence at the hands of females receive surprised remark. By far the two most violent women in Herodotus, sadists not motivated entirely by revenge, are Pheretime of Cyrene and Amestris, wife of Xerxes. These two women are violators of *nomos*, clearly monsters in Herodotus' opinion. They illustrate the historian's thesis that outrage and anomaly flourish in despotisms.

But it is a structural defect in all despotisms, including the Persian, not the sadism of one or two women, that condemns autocratic society. Family history there determines the nation's fate, and palace politics direct national policy. The despot is destined by nature to interfere in the private lives of his subjects (3.80.5*).

Women are by nature and proverbially weaker and subservient to men, below them (2.1Ω2.5; 6.77.2; 7.57.2 [?]), but any *one* might somehow break free. The significant exception, Artemisia, tyrant of Halicarnassus, who is reported to have provided the second-best fleet and the best advice to Xerxes (7.99.1), is characterized as serving with manly courage (λήματός τε καὶ ἀνδρηίης). The Persians' most

---

[14] See, e.g., as property, Helen: 2.114.2*, 115.4*, 118.3, 119.1; the lady of Cos: 9.76.2*. As machines, 2.30.4: the view of the Ethiopian deserters, which Herodotus seems to disapprove of; 5.39.2*. As victims, 2.89.2; 5.92η3* (necrophilia); 2.131.1 (Mycerinus accused of raping his daughter); 7.33 (Artaÿctes raped women in sacred precincts); 5.18.5 (Persians at Macedonian party). A glance at Xen. *Hiero* 1.26 is interesting here.

serious reproach was to call someone "worse than a woman," yet "women" is the insult that Artemisia hurls at the Persian forces at Salamis, comparing them to the Greeks in naval skills. Women are ubiquitous in Herodotus' *Histories*, but rarely do they have Artemisia's *historical* significance.

One may briefly contrast the exiguous role of women in Thucydides' *History*. One can list only six named women.[15] Thucydides thus seems to endorse Pericles' statement that the less heard of a woman for better or worse, the greater will be her standing in the community (2.45.2*). In general, women are relevant to Thucydides' text merely as examples of helpless pawns in warfare. At Plataea and in Corcyra, the ferocity and strangeness of the warfare is emphasized by the womenfolk's unusual participation in the throwing of stones and roof-tiles.[16] More often one hears of their exile (2.70.3, Potidaea) or enslavement (3.68.2 and 4.48.4, Plataea and Corcyra). Speakers mention wives and children when they conventionally exhort their soldiers to bravery (7.68. 2*, Gylippus; 69.2*, Nicias). The remarkable female wallbuilders or bread-makers for a besieged force require Thucydides' comment (5.82.6; 2.78.3). In sum, for Thucydides, women do not make history or play in it any significant role. They have a limited symbolic significance, to indicate on rare occasions the degree to which normal and expectable military activity was exceeded.[17]

Women in Herodotus, on the contrary, afford a certain expansive freedom: Candaules' wife presents a choice to Gyges where her husband had simply commanded him (1.11.2). A new realm, the private, is briefly brought into the historian's purview. Yet, women can apply or imply compulsion (ἀνάγκη): Candaules' wife demands a hasty decision; Xerxes' promised generosity forces him to concede to his mistress, against his judgement.[18] This imbroglio offers a typically indirect Herodotean way of showing "men unmanned" or "the ruler

---

[15] Chryses of Argos and her successor as priestess, Phaeinis (2.2.1; 4.133.2-3, both occasions used for chronological purposes); Hippias' daughter and wife: Archedice and Myrrhine (6.59.3, 55.1); the mythical Procne (2.29.3); and the savage Thracian Brauro, who helped kill her husband, the Edonian king (4.107.3).

[16] 2.4.2, 4; 6.4, 78.3; Corcyra: 3.74.1; cf. Argos, 5.82.6.

[17] See also Thuc. 1.103.3 (Ithome); 2.27 (Aegina); 3.36.2; 4.123.4; 5.32 (Scione), 116.4 (Melos); 7.29.4 (Mycalessus), 68.2*. See, on Thucydides' attitude towards the rules of war, D. Lateiner, "Heralds and Corpses in Thucydides," *CW* 71 (1977) 97-106.

[18] Candaules' wife: ἀναγκαίη ἐνδέειν; Xerxes: παντοῖος ἐγίνετο οὐ βουλόμενος δοῦναι.

enslaved," a motif also present in the epilogue's last words that restate the ubiquitous dichotomy of freedom and slavery. Women, and children too, provide Herodotus with a base-line, a horizon. When they rise to prominence in the story, it signals difficulties ahead for the immediate protagonist. The remarkable ones stand seductively at some threshold of good or evil, an entrance to a dangerous world. Ordinary mothers, wives, or progeny are indicators of normality, however, and furnish the reader with a standard by which one can gauge the irregularities that constitute traditional history.

IV

Our last illustration of limiting cases in Herodotus will be found in the area of moral principles. Herodotus' morality is largely cautionary. He does not preach, he represents the results of his careful collecting, selecting, and ordering of historical data.[19] He apprehends a delicate balance in the world (1.207.2*; 3.106.1), violations of which entail a restoration of balance or revenge (5.56.1 [oracle]). The balance sometimes seems to result, in the *realm of nature* especially, from "divine foresight" (3.108.2). On the human and historical level, the *nomoi* of each society (their laws and customs) provide a norm by which it can and ought to be judged.[20]

A cultural relativist, Herodotus *explicitly* recognizes the legitimacy of each society's peculiar habits (3.38; 7.152.2), but some principles he implicitly regards as universal and not to be transgressed. One prescriptive postulate may be formulated as *suum cuique*, "to each his own" (1.8.4*), or "mind your own business." Violations of this fundamental principle can disturb the natural, social, and political order. Transgressors are often severely punished by the extermination of their entire families. Perpetuation of a family, and therewith the orderly descent of property (παῖς παρὰ πατρός, 1.7.4; 2.65.3, 166.2; cf. 4.26.2), fails when men exceed their limits. This folkloristic warning is embodied in many examples of τίσις, the pervasive Herodotean theme of retribution. Limiting cases of human behavior define and establish acceptable patterns.

---

[19] How and Wells, *A Commentary on Herodotus* (Oxford 1928; repr. 1964) I, 43, complain in bold-face letters that "His history is too theological," but they hedge their complaint in the next sentence.

[20] M. Gigante, *Nomos Basileus* (Naples 1956) 115-28; S. Benardete, *Herodotean Inquiries* (The Hague 1969) 191-93; A. Cook, "Herodotus: The Act of Inquiry as a Liberation from Myth," *Helios* 3 (1976) 39-43.

Disregard for a nearly universal rule of private property, namely, exclusive possession of one's wife, opens and closes the *Histories*.[21] Initially, Candaules' love for his own wife leads him to transgress custom and urge his loyal minister Gyges to do what he should not: see his despot's wife naked. It is at once stated that "every man ought to look to his own" only: σκοπέειν τινὰ τὰ ἑωυτοῦ. Nearly the first of the aphorisms in the *Histories*, the warning will find extensive application to war and imperialism. (Professor Raubitschek has learnedly summarized the career of this aphorism.) Candaules soon lost his kingdom, dynasty, wife, family, and life.[22]

At the end of the *Histories*, the despot Xerxes desires his brother Masistes' wife and this leads him to violate law and custom. He pursued sexually his sister-in-law, and then his niece Artaÿnte (who is also his daughter-in-law). After seducing his daughter-in-law, he orders Masistes to put his wife away. His brother requests that he be allowed to keep a loyal and lawful wife, and then refuses to comply. For his insubordination, Masistes and his family are destroyed.[23] Xerxes' incestuous infatuation eventually led to his assassination at the hands of his own son, Artaÿnte's husband. To lust after another's property violates established social and political structure, be the object another's wife or all Europe.

Cyrus and Darius won empires, established law and order, and prospered. They were strategists and statesmen. Cambyses and Xerxes, who inherited their power, are less secure and often less wise about preserving it. They do not seem to know how to *look to their own*; they do not know what indeed *is* their own. Herodotus adumbrates their natures by recounting their violations of sexual morality and religious custom; these prefigure their international aggression.

One must pay back the debt that is due.[24] This will provide a related example of an illustrated principle. *Dike*, or Justice, will restore balance

[21] H. Erbse, "Der erste Satz im Werke Herodots," in *Festschrift Bruno Snell* (Munich 1956) 220: Herodotus begins and ends his work with despotic arbitrariness. Immerwahr (above, note 4: 1966) 43: "The work begins and ends at points that are not at all arbitrary." In history, all divisions, especially beginnings, are in some sense arbitrarily chosen, but Herodotus' are certainly not without point or purpose.

[22] 1.8.1,4*; χρῆν γὰρ Κανδαύλῃ γενέσθαι κακῶς, 1.8.2; 1.12.2. For the aphorism, see A.E. Raubitschek, "Ein neues Pittakeion," *WS* 71 (1958) 170-72; cf. idem, "Die schamlose Ehefrau," *Rh M* 100 (1957) 139-40.

[23] 9.108.1-2; 9.111.4.

[24] 5.99.1, ὀφειλόμενά σφι ἀποδιδόντες; Athenians succor Milesians. Cf. Xerxes' wrathful comment to Masistes (9.111.5*): μάθῃς τὰ διδόμενα δέκεσθαι.

(Anaximander F 1), will right wrongs, not uncommonly by a special form of *tisis*, revenge, namely by the extirpation of the house of the wicked.

Seven men are noticed as *childless*, at least in the male line, in Herodotus. This reflects Greek concern for continuity of the family. Five of these seven are strongly condemned. King Astyages who tried to kill his grandson Cyrus, a crime against universal custom of blood-ties and inheritance, was overthrown and incarcerated.[25] Cambyses' crimes were legion. His incest with two of his sisters[26] and murder of one, and his senseless imperial aggression, seem to cause him to die ἄπαις, childless.[27] Cleomenes, a victim of Herodotus' hostile sources, is falsely said to have reigned but briefly, but he is correctly reported as childless in the male line.[28] Both misfortunes serve presumably as retribution for his political improprieties. The elder Miltiades and his nephew Stesagoras both die without children. Some curse afflicted the family, or at least Herodotus' informants may have wished to think so. Artaÿctes and his only son meet violent torture and barbaric death (9.120.4), fit for a man deemed guilty of the most monstrous crimes.[29] Herodotus confirms the principle of *tisis* and employs little subtlety in connecting problems of perpetuation with deeds of extraordinary wickedness. The childlessness of Phoenix, a punishment sent by the gods, offered sufficient Homeric precedent (*Iliad* 9.453-57, 492-95).

One's children comprise one's everything (7.224.2); genocidal destruction is obviously the worst fate imaginable.[30] The dreadful baking and stewing of Harpagus' son by Astyages, incidentally ending the former's family line, *justifies* his subsequent treason, his betrayal of the entire Median empire to the Persians.

[25] 1.109.3*, 130.3. His punishment of Harpagus inflicts on that unwilling man the extirpation of the very heirs that he had sought for himself. Harpagus' revenge in effect serves to put the vizier in Astyages' position as Cyrus' creator (savior).

[26] Herodotus notes both that his younger sister had the same two parents, and that incestuous unions were not a Persian custom (3.31.1-2). Next-of-kin marriage was, in fact, a common feature of Zoroastrianism.

[27] 3.31.1-2, 38.1, 66.2.

[28] 5.48; 7.205.1; cf. How and Wells (above, note 19) II, app. xvii, 347-53., esp. 347-8.

[29] ἀθέμιστα (7.33), ἀτάσθαλος (9.116.1). He had sexually violated women on sacred ground and lied to his King. His son was stoned to death before his eyes prior to his own crucifixion. Pindar contrarily celebrates good deeds and a consequent confidence in generational *kleos* and survival: *Nem.* 7.100-101: παίδων δὲ παῖδες ἔχοιεν αἰεὶ /γέρας; *Oly.* 8.70-71: πατρὶ δὲ πατρὸς ἐνέπνευσεν μένος γήραος ἀντίπαλον.

[30] Croesus threatened Lampsacus thus (6.37, esp. 37.2).

Two mini-dramas even more explicitly show that οὐδεὶς ἀνθρώπων ἀδικῶν τίσιν οὐκ ἀποτίσει ("Every man will pay back the debt for his wrongs," 5.56.1 [oracle]). Panionius made his fortune castrating young men. A certain Hermotimus was one of his victims. Hermotimus eventually became the most trusted eunuch of Xerxes. One day he lured his Greek mutilator into bringing his whole family into his power.[31] Thereupon accusing him of "deeds most unholy" and asserting that his capture had been, and his punishment would be, by divine dispensation, he forced wretched Panionius to castrate all four of his own sons, and then compelled the sons to do the same to the father. Herodotus characterizes this action (8.105.1, cf. 106.4) as "the greatest vengeance (*tisis*) indeed of all we know that ever befell someone who had been wronged." The deed may be monstrous, but Herodotus does not disapprove. He records it as a warning.

Finally, the folktale of Glaucus the Spartan told by Leutychidas at Athens (6.86a-δ*) provides material for one of those dramatic speeches that interpret events and clarify the issues that Herodotus thinks significant.[32] Glaucus was universally esteemed for his just dealing (*dikaiosyne, ter*). A Milesian entrusted to him on oath a large sum of money (*paratheke*), because Sparta was stable whereas Ionia was always exposed to danger and financial uncertainty. Glaucus did *not* pay back as agreed. When he asked for advice, the Pythia rebuked him saying that Oath has an anonymous child who destroys perjurors and their progeny. He who profits by theft will have no offspring, no family (*oikos*) at all, for Oath's son will blot them out, while the man who abides by his oath will have blessed progeny (*genee*). The character Leutychidas here offers what the author Herodotus generally shrinks from; he tells us what to make of his fable: "Why I've told you this story will now be stated: Of Glaucus now there is no descendant (*apogonos*) whatsoever, nor is there any family thought to be related to Glaucus. Indeed he has been wiped out root and branch (*prorrhizos*)." Only thrice, in exceptionally significant narratives, does Herodotus employ the word *prorrhizos*: Solon's warning to Croesus, Amasis' warning to Polycrates,[33] and here. In all these cases, great good fortune

---

[31] 8.106.2-3, τὰ τέκνα καὶ τὴν γυναῖκα ... πανοικίη. Note the use of direct speech.

[32] L. Solmsen, "Speeches in Herodotus' Account of the Ionian Revolt," *AJP* 64 (1943) 194-95; eadem, "Speeches in Herodotus' Account of the Battle of Plataea," *CP* 39 (1944) 242, 253; Ch. Fornara, *Herodotus: An Interpretive Essay* (Oxford 1971) 22; even A.H. Sayce, *The Ancient Empires of the East* (London 1883) xxv.

[33] 1.32.9*; 3.40.3*. Croesus' line ends with himself since Atys dies, and, by his own reckoning, his other son was of no account (3.34.3*). On this word, cf. Wolf Aly,

is dangerous; it leads men to acts that destroy them and their progeny. Glaucus' gratuitous misdeed points the moral: the principle of "from father to son,"[34] the perpetuation of family and family property, fails when propriety is ignored. Privileged vocabulary, subject, and repeated patterns of historical action demonstrate that notions of boundaries and their violation characterize Herodotus' composition.

V

The East Aegean historian probably was acquainted with contemporary medical research and theory. *On the Nature of the Child* would use the special term ἱστόριον for visible evidence from which valid inferences may be made (ch. 31; *Epid.* IV.54). Herodotus also had evidence from which valid inferences could be drawn. A determined empiricism, analogies, limited generalizations, a critical spirit, structuring concepts, an indefinable liveliness—what von Fritz calls *historische Lebendigkeit*—these are essential elements, not intrusions, in Herodotus' unimitated invention. He calls it, assertively, ἱστορίης ἀπόδεξις "a demonstration of his research." When we recognize his literary habits and structuring techniques, his text and its meanings become more easily accessible. Certainly we shall have advanced our comprehension beyond the assumption that Herodotus wanted to be what modern historians are!

Herodotus, despite his cautious agnosticism, made mistakes and was gulled on occasion, but he saw what was essential (7.139), and what was at stake in the Persian Wars. Yet he always manages to respect the particularity of events; he *reports* the contingent rather than explains it—away. He hovers precariously between the particular and the general. Here he is unique. He varies genre and tone: by turns he is tragic, comic, exotic, and erotic. His modes of presentation differ: narrative and speech, folktale, fiction, and bald narrative. His method is expansive and experimental.

What he had recorded did not make him an optimist about man's narrow capacities to learn. His relentless curiosity and intelligent diligence, stimulated by the life of a refugee, united to leave us—to paraphrase the author—"a work great and worthy of wonder that will never be forgotten."

Volksmärchen, Sage und Novelle bei Herodot und seinen Zeitgenossen (Göttingen 1921; repr. 1969) 91, note 1.

[34] παῖς παρὰ πατρός: 1.7.4; 2.65.3; 2.166.2.

Persians in Herodotus

DAVID M. LEWIS
Christ Church, Oxford University

Toni was one of my first graduate teachers when I arrived in 1951 at what, after two years in the army, seemed only just this side of paradise, and he has been a steady support and solace ever since. It is the greatest possible pleasure to join in his birthday celebration.

This is not a wide-ranging investigation of Herodotus' interest in or attitude to the Persian Empire or the Persian character. The questions involved are about Herodotus the investigator and narrator, and are not new. They concern the methods by which he was able to know so much about that empire, and they involve the oldest questions of all: How much trouble did he take in the search for truth? Did he in fact have any conscience about the truth at all?

Historians are not unaware that Herodotus' truthfulness has been challenged from time to time, but on the whole they take no notice. To speak frankly, they have to ignore such criticisms or be put out of business, particularly when dealing with Persian history. Historians abhor a vacuum, and narrative sources on the Persian side are virtually non-existent. We only have the Babylonian texts which cover Cyrus' occupation of Babylon and the Behistun Inscription to cover the accession year of Darius. The result is that, if one is to write a narrative account of the reigns of Darius and Xerxes at all, there is no alternative to using Herodotus' narrative as the core of that account. The assumption has to be that Herodotus is right, except when he can be shown to be wrong; that is a principle which is carried into many other aspects of near eastern studies besides straight narrative. If you start with the postulate that you should use no Herodotus unless he can be shown to be right, you just won't get very far. That would be an inconvenient line, but not intellectually disreputable. It would be more disreputable to get caught, say, in the position of saying that Herodotus' account of Babylon is factually wrong, but must nevertheless be atmospherically accurate.

In this situation, any new opportunity for testing Herodotus' accuracy against outside sources must be taken, in the hope of determining where the probabilities lie for any given body of material. I think that such a new opportunity now exists, and I shall be exploring it this morning.

That Herodotus had some very good sources about Persia has been clear since the decipherment of the Behistun Inscription. The main lines of his account of Darius' accession were clearly very similar to that of Behistun. Specifically, his list of the helpers of Darius in the assassination of the false Smerdis came out very well indeed. Unlike the epitome of Ktesias, who claimed to have been using official records, but only got one and a half names out of six right, Herodotus only got one wrong, naming Aspathines instead of, apparently, Ardumaniŝ. Even in naming Aspathines, he had some excuse, since Aspathines was unquestionably important later in Darius' reign, being named as quiver-bearer of the King on Darius' tomb, the only person besides Gobryas to be so named. The other prosopographical weakness is that he makes Otanes the son of Pharnaspes, and I can think of no way of making that correspond to Behistun's Θuxra.

It is clear of course that there is no question of Herodotus having used a written text of Behistun. But he might well have found one had he looked for it. Though the inscription itself was only in Old Persian, Elamite and Babylonian, there were other versions: §70 "Afterwards this inscription I sent off everywhere among the provinces. The people unitedly worked upon it." If the Jews of Elephantine in southern Egypt had a copy in Aramaic at the end of the fifth century (this was a copy of an older manuscript), I would positively expect, considering the number of Darius' Greek-speaking subjects, that there was at some stage a Greek text, and I occasionally look hopefully at some of the scrappier late sixth century Greek inscriptions of Asia

Minor in the hope of finding a fragment. But there is in fact no trace of Behistun having influenced a Greek historian, unless you include the unaccountable fact that Justin (I.9.7) calls one of the usurping Magi Cometes, which, considering the transmission-process, is not a bad shot at Gaumata.

Herodotus is broadly right on the names, and roughly right on the length of the usurpation. But he seems to have no knowledge of the claims to royal legitimacy which Darius puts forward and treats him as an ordinary Achaemenid. He gets various minor details wrong, like the place where the Magi were killed. Above all, he has virtually no knowledge, in this context, of the extensive revolts which surrounded Darius' accession and which occupy so much of the Behistun Inscription.

His account of the accession, therefore, comes through an intermediary, and it has never played as prominent a part in the search for specific sources for his Persian information as three passages where the chances of a documentary basis have always seemed fairly high, the list of provinces or, rather, financial districts at III.89 ff., the description of the Royal Road at V.52-54, and the account of Xerxes' army and its commanders at VII.61-98. These documents have not escaped criticism. The list of provinces has repeatedly been compared with lists issued by Darius and Xerxes themselves. Most of the discrepancies can be explained away if one thinks, with Cameron,[1] that their lists are simply lists of peoples, without administrative pretensions, but there are one or two awkwardnesses towards the east of the empire. There have always been some who have doubted whether the Royal Road really went that way, but, as far as I can judge, there is no real obstacle to believing that it describes at least part of the imperial road system. The list of Xerxes' forces is a more complex matter, which will be occupying us more and more in this lecture. The temptation has been felt to treat the whole list as a compilation from an ethnographic base, a literary invention to match the Homeric Catalogue of Ships, carrying the implication, which some have found incredible, that Xerxes was accompanied by men from all his peoples. I can say now that I shall eventually be accepting part of the case against this list, but that I find no serious difficulty in believing that the bare facts about contingents and commanders were available in

[1] G.G. Cameron, "The Persian Satrapies and Related Matters," *JNES* 32 (1973) 47 ff.

a documentary source. Such a list, it was claimed by the Alexander-historian Aristoboulos (Arr. *Anab*. III.11.3), was in fact found in the Persian camp after the battle of Gaugamela. If it turns out that we can increase our faith in at any rate the names of the commanders, we shall thereby be increasing our belief in Herodotus' ability to get reliable information. If we lose faith in these, the most documentary-looking, parts of Herodotus' account of Persia, the sceptics are fully entitled to their point of view.

Herodotus does give some indications of his sources, but even these may be doubted. Detlev Fehling, in a 1971 book[2] which is perhaps gaining in influence, attempted to establish the proposition that, in any case in which Herodotus names his source, this is an infallible sign that he had no direct source. There is more to be said for this proposition than you may think, and its destructive effect is in practice modified by the fact that, although for Fehling the amount of invention in Herodotus is very considerable, he is willing to agree that Herodotus does not always make things up out of nothing at all. Despite Fehling's doubts, I should perhaps say something about what Herodotus says about his sources. By and large, he has certainly left us with the impression that his sources for Persian affairs are Persian. His account of Cyrus goes back to those Persians who do not want to exaggerate (I.95.1). That the Persians give two versions of why Darius' horse neighed (III.87) carries the implication that the narrative of Darius' accession is all Persian, and there is a similar allusion to what Persians say about Darius at III.89.3 just as the list of provinces starts. Thereafter we get remarkably little, but a continued attempt to suggest authentic Persian information comes out in a touch like "Masistios, whom the Greeks call Makistios" (IX.20). Clearly all this does not add up to much, and, Fehling or no Fehling, the question of sources remains pretty open.

The search for Herodotus' sources for Persian affairs has been actively pursued, but it has mostly been conducted under the influence of a strange presupposition that there was a political and linguistic iron curtain between Greeks and Persians. It has therefore been thought necessary and desirable to look for very specific holes in this curtain through which Herodotus' information might have come. I do not think that Herodotus himself supports this attitude. We will recall that he lays stress on one point in Egyptian history where the

---

[2] Detlev Fehling, *Die Quellenangaben bei Herodot* (Berlin 1971).

presence of Greeks starts (II.154.4): "with these people settled in Egypt, the Greeks mixed with them and we know exactly everything which happened in Egypt starting with Psammetichus and later on." This is not an excessive claim, and no one doubts the great superiority of Herodotus' coverage of the 26th Dynasty over his earlier Egyptian history. He makes no such claim for Persia, and the Greeks who first come into contact with Darius in his pages, Demokedes the doctor and Maiandrios the Samian exile, are there for their relevance to the development of Persian aggression against Greece. He draws no dividing line here about information, and I don't think that it occurred to him that he had to. The arrival of Maiandrios is surprising to Darius because he personally is new to the throne and no Greeks have yet called on him. There is, however, a staff of interpreters ready to elucidate the matter (III.140.2-3); there is no parallel between this scene and the Assyrian texts of the 650s in which the messenger of Gyges of Lydia found no one at Assurbanipal's court who could understand his language.

Nevertheless, the tendency has been to look for the most obvious breaches of this supposed iron curtain, and some names have been fashionable from time to time. We do not hear much nowadays of the memoirs of Dikaios the Athenian exile (VIII.65). He at least has the merit of having told a story, but we do not know to whom he told it. Other guesses have only seemed plausible to their authors; the most recent[3] is the eunuch of Sataspes who ran away to Samos (IV.43 fin.). Some have had longer runs. There is quite a lot to be said for the exiled Spartan king Demaratos. At least we know that he had accessible descendants in the Kaikos valley, and there is even some reason to believe that Herodotus had been there (II.10.1). He is perhaps a rather more attractive source for dissensions in the Persian high command than for administrative detail. But the overwhelmingly favoured candidate has always been Zopyros son of Megabyxos, who, according to Herodotus himself, ran away from Persia to Athens at dates variously estimated as the late 440s or the early 420s.

I am not a Zopyros man myself and am sustained in that by my belief that the story for which he would be the most obvious source, his grandfather's services in the recapture of Babylon (III.150-160), appears on the face of it to be a pack of lies. This Babylonian revolt

[3] Dolores Hegyi, "The Historical Authenticity of Herodotus in the Persian Logoi," *Acta Antiqua Academiae Scientiarum Hungaricae* 21 (1973) 73 ff.

is said to come very early in Darius' reign, but really the only point of resemblance between it and either of those of 521 described by the Behistun inscriptions is that it ends with 3,000 Babylonian nobles being impaled on stakes; the second Babylonian revolt in the Behistun inscription ends with nobles being impaled on stakes, the total of those killed in battle and surviving of the whole army being 2,497.[4] Such things must have happened not infrequently (Darius had impaled 49 the year before), and the coincidence does not seem to be sufficiently strong to outweigh the facts, 1) that it was Intaphernes whom the inscription credits with the capture of Babylon, 2) that the Babylonian revolts of 522/1 lasted two and a half and three months and not twenty, 3) that there is no Babylonian evidence that grandfather Zopyros was ever governor of Babylon, 4) that the kind of thing which Herodotus says about the fate of Babylon seems to fit much better what happened to Babylon in the early years of Xerxes (though even here we cannot fit in a siege of twenty months). In fact, this is the one place where they coincide, in which there is any temptation to prefer Ktesias to Herodotus. Ktesias does have a siege of Babylon early in Xerxes' reign. If Zopyros was Herodotus' source for all this, there is not much incentive to make him a source for the documents.

Let us start again. At some time not long after 493 a very large number of clay tablets was removed from the offices of the ration-administration at Persepolis and dumped in the construction of the fortification wall at the north-east corner of the Persepolis terrace. They did not reemerge until 1933-34 and, for excellent linguistic reasons, only one of them was published before 1969. We now have published texts of over 2,100,[5] relevant in various ways to the movement and disbursement of food stuffs in the area from 510 to 493. On grounds of scale alone, this is by far the most substantial accretion to our documentary knowledge of the Persian Empire in this century. They are not the only documentary texts from Persepolis. A

---

[4] Those who are most familiar with the Bisitun inscription in its Old Persian version seem not to realize that the Babylonian and Aramaic versions add casualty figures. For the Babylonian version, see E.N. von Voigtlander, *The Bisitun Inscription of Darius the Great, Babylonian Version (Corpus Inscriptionum Iranicarum*, Part I, Volume II i, London 1978). For the Aramaic version, see J.C. Greenfield and P. Porten, *The Bisitun Inscription of Darius the Great, Aramaic Version (Corpus Inscriptionum Iranicarum*, Part I, Volume V i, London 1982).

[5] R.T. Hallock, *Persepolis Fortification Tablets (OIP* 92, Chicago 1969) from which individual texts are cited with the prefix PF, supplemented by *Cahiers de la Délégation française en Iran* 8 (1978) 109 ff. from which individual texts are cited with the prefix PFa.

smaller group, about 130, of tablets similar in language and appearance was never dumped but remained in the treasury until Alexander came; they record disbursements of silver for a slightly later period, 492 to 458.[6] Many fields for investigation are thus opened, but I shall be trying today, on a fairly narrow front, to see what the finds do for our appreciation of Herodotus.

Two main points seem to emerge. The first is straightforward. We now have an enormous increase in our body of facts about the reigns of Darius and, to a lesser extent, that of Xerxes. As far as Herodotus is concerned, the preponderance of relevant facts is prosopographic, and this gives us a chance of making further tests on the extraordinarily rich material which he is able to produce about the Persian leadership.

The second is more indirect. The bulk of the tablets is in the isolated language of Elamite, heavily penetrated with Persian loan-words. Some of them also bore notes in Aramaic, no doubt made by those of the secretarial staff who are also described as Babylonian scribes, writers on parchment; there are some unpublished tablets in Aramaic as well. One tablet was in Phrygian. One of them, however, was in Greek, recording a transfer of wine. To simplify a long story, it results from the fact that there was at least one person in about 500 out on the administrative circuit to whom it came most naturally to write in Greek and who knew that there was someone in the central office who would be able to cope with it. The search for such persons is not a long one. No one has ever doubted that the Elamite word for Greeks is Yaunā-ip, and they are not infrequent in our documents, whether they are engaged in transporting building materials or employed more menially, like the twenty-three ladies who Hallock, the publisher of the tablets, thought were irrigation-workers and whom Hinz[7] more reasonably translates as 'spinsters'. (Since they are getting bonus rations for producing children, it should be clear that I use the word in its primary sense.) There are men in our texts who are simply called Yaunā. No one that I know of has spoken against the obvious view that this is not a true proper name, that the persons concerned are Greeks, known by their ethnics instead of their strange and no doubt unpronounceable names, just as the Greeks habitually called slaves Skythes or Kar. One is not all that high up, a grain-handler on an out-station in 503 and 502. The other two are.

---

[6] G.G. Cameron, *Persepolis Treasury Texts* (*OIP* 65, Chicago 1948) from which individual texts are cited with the prefix PT.

[7] W. Hinz, *Neue Wege im Altpersischen* (Wiesbaden 1973) 95.

One of them was from December 499 to September 498 the only visible aide-de-camp of Parnaka, the uncle of the King and chief economic official of Persis; the other, if he be another, is found early in 481 in the same position with the high official Artatakma. They are transmitting the high official's orders to the scribes who will actually write them down. They only dictate so they do not need to be literate themselves in Elamite; they do need to have enough spoken Persian and Elamite to do their jobs. On these facts, I argued a few years ago[8] that if we find Greeks in a secretarial capacity as early as this and as far east as this, there should be no reason to doubt their availability to the King, and to satraps, particularly in the west, in all relevant periods. None of my reviewers has objected and I hope that I can take this as reasonably established.

The consequence for today should be obvious. There was no iron curtain. It seems demonstrable that the Persian administration employed Greeks at a level where certain kinds of information would be easily accessible to them, and this information could include general Persian information. Such people were not employed merely to write down the names of Greek trierarchs, though we certainly need them for Herodotus' list at VIII.85.2. There have been occasional references in the literature to the possibility of Herodotus' sources including them. They now seem to me to be very strong candidates indeed, and I think we have increased the chances of Herodotus having been able to acquire information.

That he could have done is not the same as saying that he did. To estimate the chances of that we need to look at the actual information which Persepolis provides. For those of my friends who may reasonably doubt the thoroughness of my knowledge of Old Persian and Elamite, I think I can say that I shall not be using many equivalences which have not also been used by Rudiger Schmitt[9] for purely onomastic purposes.

We have to start by understanding the nature of the evidence which the tablets are bringing to our knowledge of the Persian upper-classes between 510 and 493. Some of the evidence is fairly straightforward. We can tell whether a person is important because of the range of

---

[8] D.M. Lewis, *Sparta and Persia* (*Cincinnati Classical Studies* 1, Leiden 1977) 12-15.
[9] R. Schmitt, "The Medo-Persian Names of Herodotus in the Light of the New Evidence from Persepolis," *Acta Antiqua Academiae Scientiarum Hungaricae* 24 (1976) 25 ff.

his interests and also if he receives unusually large rations of commodities. But the bulk of the evidence comes from the travel-documents. The Elamite form of the Old Persian for these is *miyatukka*, linguistically equivalent to the word *viaticum* which still exists today in a fairly specialized context. These are sealed documents ensuring the right of their holder to receive rations as he passes along the Royal Road. It is clear that the right to issue these documents is a function of the king or of someone at satrapal level; in two cases satraps seem to have deputies who can do it. By observing the direction of the journeys authorized, we can localize these satraps. The documents therefore enormously increase our knowledge of Darius' satraps, providing us with what looks like his uncle, Pharnakes the son of Arsames, mostly, though not always, in Persepolis, where he has a deputy Ziššawiš, a Megabanos satrap in Susa (and his deputy Mardunda), an Artabanos satrap in Bactria, Megabazos in Arachosia/Gandara/Parikania, Artabawa in India, Hydarnes in Media, and satraps in Areia and Carmania. A few other people are not so easy to locate. That list should indicate the limitations of our evidence. Persepolis is the furthest east of the Empire's capitals, and journeys to it are more likely to come from eastern areas; even for Babylon we only have one journey to it and none from it; the stray people who come from Sardis are very unusual. Journeys from the western provinces are much more likely to end in Susa. This means that, since Herodotus' interests are inevitably fixed on the western side of the empire, the correlations are likely to be reduced. Correspondingly, the tablets give us people in the east of some importance who do not appear in Herodotus at all. This is a handicap, but working with the texts gives me reasonable assurance that most of the people in Herodotus must be real people. If one tries to correlate the names in Aeschylus or in Ktesias (for this period; he gets better later in the century), one gets a very sharp contrast and is left feeling that their names are merely vaguely oriental. A much lower proportion is directly translatable into Elamite or Persian.

I start with straight cases where Herodotus' information is confirmed.

1) The most obvious one is that he makes Darius' full brother Artaphernes satrap of Sardis, where he stays, say, from 511 to 493. An Irdapirna issues travel warrants, one of which (PF 1404) is explicitly for a journey from Sardis to Persepolis in November 495.

2) In III.88 Darius marries Artystone, daughter of Cyrus. In the army-list at VII.69.2 further information is given about her. Her sons Arsames (ibid.) and Gobryas (72.2) are named as commanders, and she is said to be Darius' favourite wife. Irtašduna, twice qualified as *dukšiš*, appears on 25 Elamite texts, as a recipient of rations, as an owner of fairly small numbers of workers, and giving orders for the issue of provisions from her estate, from March 503 to some time in 497. The two earliest texts show the King authorizing the issue to her of 100 sheep and 200 *marriš* (say 1,940 liters) of wine, perhaps for a special feast, and at least one more text (PF 718) shows him closely concerned in her affairs. Three texts of 498 (PF 733-4,2035) associate her with Iršama, who must be her son Arsames. Arsames in his turn (PF 309,498) orders the supply of grain to a woman called Uparmiya. She has been taken for his wife; there is more temptation to identify her with his stepmother, Parmis, daughter of Smerdis, another wife of Darius (III.88.3, VII.78).

3) I come now to an older Gobryas. For Herodotus, he is, correctly, one of the Seven (III.70,73,78), and with Darius on the Scythian expedition (IV.132,134). Thereafter he does not appear in person. Later references (VII.2.2, 97) tell us that Darius had been married to Gobryas' daughter before he came to the throne and that Gobryas had married Darius' sister, by whom he had a son Mardonios (VII.5.1). Strictly speaking, Herodotus does not identify his Gobryases, but the Behistun inscription tells us that the Gobryas of the Seven was son of Mardonios, which is comforting. Mardonios makes his first appearance in 493 (VI.43.1) as commander in the West; he is young and has recently married Darius' daughter Artazostra. His campaign is a disaster; he loses his fleet off Mount Athos, is himself wounded in Thrace and goes off home. He is not employed by Darius on the Marathon campaign, which has new commanders, of whom more later. His next appearance is after Xerxes' accession (VII.5.1) where he is the man who has the greatest influence with Xerxes. He is consistently presented as the most zealous advocate of the invasion of Greece, as against the King's uncle Artabanos. He makes light of difficulties, tells lies about his own previous campaign (VII.9.2), and keeps on going, in 480 as the first-named of the six land-marshals (VII.82), in 479 as the principal commander.

There has not been any doubt that Herodotus has, if anything, underplayed the importance of Gobryas. After the murder of the false

Smerdis, he has a later command against Elam in the Behistun inscription, and, as spear-bearer of the King, is one of the only two Persians to be both portrayed and named on Darius' tomb. This position will account for the rapid promotion of Mardonios, though we note that it is not Artobarzanes, Gobryas' grandson (VII.2.2) but Xerxes who wins the succession to Darius. Artobarzanes turns up twice at Persepolis as a satrap, but we cannot locate him (PF 1463, 2052).

The tablets help further. Kambarma (the Elamite form of Gobryas) turned up on them relatively early (PF 688). In March 498 he was receiving a beer-ration of 100 quarts a day, 11% higher than the next highest liquid ration known. It now appears (PFa 5) that he was on that occasion meeting an unnamed lady, described as 'wife of Mardonios, daughter of the King'; she has an appropriately high flourration, the second highest known. The family party in that month is now completed by a lady Radušnamuya (PF 684), with a wine-ration of 44 quarts a day; an unpublished tablet describes her as 'of Gobryas the...' Presumably she is his wife, Darius' daughter and Mardonios' mother.

Herodotus is thus confirmed on Mardonios' marriage, though not, apparently, on the chronology. For us, March 498 is not very recent in 493. I do not know whether this is a fact about his information or about his use of νεωστί, a point which has been more warmly debated in connection with the career of Themistocles.

So much for the positive correlations. Negative correlations, of the type provided by Behistun, are not really to be expected; our documents are not like that. It would only be fair to say, since I have already said something about the great ladies, that it has proved distressingly difficult to find Atossa, daughter of Cyrus, wife of Darius, mother of Xerxes. There are other women about in the tablets, closely comparable to Artystone, above all Irdabama and Abbamuš, but it is not easy to make them into Atossa. The first thought was that she was dead before the tablets started, but Hinz, who suggested this, immediately withdrew it on the grounds that Aeschylus proved that she was alive in 480.[10] There is of course no evidence in Aeschylus' text that he knew the name or anything about her. I should attach more importance to Herodotus' belief (VII.3.4) that she was around

[10] *Orientalia* 39 (1970) 423; *ZAssyr* 61 (1971) 291.

at the time that Darius designated Xerxes as his heir, but of course this is the sort of thing one could be agnostic about.

If you want negative correlations for Herodotus' oriental prosopography, you have to go outside the tablets and indeed outside the Persians. Straightforward reading of VII.98 and VIII.67 suggests that he thought that the King of Sidon in 480 was called Tetramnestos son of Anysos. Neither of these names looks very like Esmunazar or Tabnit, which seem to be the relevant royal names in Sidon at the time.[11] Escape-routes have been tried and are available, but we should not start from the postulate that Herodotus must be right. A similar situation arises with the Lycian of VII.98, *Κυβέρνισκος Σίκα* or, better, *Κύβερνις Κοσσίκα*. There are coins with *Κυ* and *Κυβ*, but there are difficulties about the end of the name, and the more we know about the Lycian dynasty, the more awkward the middle of *Κοσσίκα* looks.[12]

I pass now to points where the tablets provide information consistent with Herodotus in a way which makes his information sound more plausible. The first is rather picturesque. Darius, at the start of his reign, wishes to remove Oroites the satrap of Sardis, and this is ingeniously achieved by Bagaios the son of Artontes (III.127-8). This ought to get a suitable reward, but Herodotus says nothing. You will remember that Artystone was labeled *dukšiš*. This ought to mean something like 'princess', and that has been recently confirmed by its appearance (PFa 31:13) qualifying ladies named as daughters of Hystaspes, who ought to be sisters of Darius; they have enormous beer-rations. One other *dukšiš* remains, Ištin (PF 823), who receives two sheep together with Bakeya, who I assume is her husband. That ought to be Bagaios. In other lands one gets half the kingdom as well as a princess for notable service, but that is hardly possible in Persia. At the risk of running ahead of my chronology, I draw attention to Mardontes son of Bagaios, commander of Red Sea islanders in 480 (VII.80) and one of three fleet-commanders in 479 (VIII.130.2, IX.102). This may well be the same Bagaios, since grandson and grandfather will share a name-element, and there is a very suitable identification with Mardunda, deputy satrap in Susa in 499-494.

With one prominent exception, which I defer, no very plausible identifications appear for most of Darius' commanders in the west,

[11] Galling, *ZDPV* 79 (1963) 150 n.51; Dunand, *MelUSJ* 49 (1975/76) 495.
[12] J. Bousquet, "Arbinas, fils de Gergis, Dynaste de Xanthos," *CRAI* 1975 142 note 12.

though most of the names can be readily rendered into Elamite. Nothing makes the identification of Daurises, Hymaies and Otanes (V.116) with people of the same name more than possible. There is the occasional possibility of reversing the process. An isolated high personage, who cannot be placed geographically, called Ziššamakka (PF 1493; December 500) was treated by Hallock as a by-form of the well-known Ziššawiš. This was unnecessary. Consider the Sisimakes (Sisamakes, Sisamankes, Susamankes) who gets killed in high command, say in 497 (V.121).

I have already published[13] a contribution to the history of the Ionian revolt. Herodotus has no knowledge of the career of Datis before his appointment to command the Marathon campaign of 490, though he knows that he is a Mede. It had been guessed that he ought to have had some previous experience before his collaboration with Darius' young nephew Artaphernes, and a stray reference in the Lindian Temple Chronicle has been used to support a guess that he was a commander in 494, a year in which Herodotus gives no fleet commander. Publishing a tablet concerning one Datiya with the high beer-ration of 70 quarts, I argued that this was Datis, on his way back from Sardis in January 494 from a mission to report to Darius on the Ionian Revolt.

I now turn to the names in the catalogue of Xerxes' army. By now, we are thirteen years after the last Fortification Tablet, but it is clearly not unlikely that at least the senior people in 480 will be visible at Persepolis in some capacity.

Starting from the top, the six marshals of VII.82, we begin with three of Xerxes' cousins, Mardonios, Tritantaichmes and Smerdomenes. Mardonios we have already met, but no new light is thrown on Tritantaichmes or Smerdomenes, or indeed on the fourth marshal, Masistes, Xerxes' full brother. The fifth marshal, Gergis son of Ariazos or Arizos, has always been enigmatic, with no visible high connections to fit him for his grand company. Burn[14] suggests that he may be the indispensable master of detail, the adjutant- and quartermaster-general, although he does not visibly behave as such, and finds it interesting that someone from outside the Seven Houses should rise so high. It is therefore comforting to be able to suggest an identification. Travel-authorizations give us a Karkiš, satrap of

[13] D.M. Lewis, "Datis the Mede," *JHS* 100 (1980) 194-5.
[14] A.R. Burn, *Persia and the Greeks* (London 1962) 323.

Carmania at least from 501 to 494, and that looks quite a plausible 'praetorian' province for an able man on his way up in a career based on talent. There is nothing implausible about his father's name. It will correspond to Elamite Harriyazza which comes twice, though not for high personages. The sixth marshal is Megabyxos son of Zopyros, safely attributable to one of the Seven Houses. He has recently been claimed[15] as *the* great Persian military innovator. Surviving into the 440s, he will be on the young side in 480. Persepolis only produces an undated 'companion of Bagapukša' on a slightly abnormal ration-scale (PF 1255).

On this level we can put the commander of the Immortals, Hydarnes son of Hydarnes (VII.83); whether he also held a coastal command in Asia and when (VII.135), need not detain us. He clearly should be the son of Hydarnes of the Seven; that *he* was satrap of Media until at least 499, I have argued elsewhere.[16] There is another possible son, commander of the Arians in VII.66.1, Sisamnes son of Hydarnes, but the name is not uncommon, at various levels.

I pass now to the hipparchs (VII.88). One of them, Pharnuches, had an accident and was left behind, which left Harmamithres and Tithaios, sons of Datis. Herodotus does not say that this is *the* Datis, but it is clearly not unlikely. Datis was a Mede, Media was a horse-rearing country, and some have found him taking a special interest in cavalry on the Marathon campaign. I can offer nothing on Harmamithres beyond the fact that Harma- is a Persian name-element, but I do find some interest in Tithaios. Old Persian roots in Ciça, Ciθra produce Elamite forms in Zišša, and a whole range of Greek equivalents Τισσα, Τριτα, Τιθρα, Τιθα, Σισ. So Tithaios ought to come out as Elamite Ziššaya or something like it. There is no difficulty in finding a candidate here. The single most frequent character in the Persepolis tablets is Ziššawiš, spelt in fourteen different ways, and the nearest Greek equivalent to that is certainly Τιθαῖος. Ziššawiš is a principal functionary at Persepolis from August 504 to February 467. Seldom quite at the top, he is nevertheless substantial. He uses a seal of Darius himself. We have no evidence for his rations after 499, but even then, when he must be quite young, he is on 1½ sheep, 60 quarts of flour and 30 of wine a day. I do not speculate on the

[15] P.A. Rahe, "The Military Situation in Western Asia on the Eve of Cunaxa," *AJP* 101 (1980) 88-9.

[16] Lewis (supra note 8) 84 note 14.

dynasty's use of Medes, but this seems a suitable career for an important one.

Now the admirals (VII.97). These start with Ariabignes, Xerxes' half-brother, and Achaimenes, his full brother. Neither of these has yet turned up at Persepolis. The third is Prexaspes son of Aspathines. I said before that Aspathines was not one of the Seven, although Herodotus thought that he was, but that Herodotus was partly excused by the fact that Aspathines was eventually very important with Darius, appearing on his tomb as quiver-bearer. At Persepolis Aspathines appears late in the Fortification Tablets in 494 and early in the Treasury Tablets in 483. He is the most obvious successor, if we look for a single one, for the King's uncle Parnaka as Ziššawiš' superior in charge of Persepolis. The inscription on his seal has been read[17] as "son of Prexaspes." If this is right, this would make the connection back to the Prexaspes who plays a somewhat equivocal role in Herodotus' third book, but gets a good press for it, and forward to this admiral. Even if it is not right, there is clearly sufficient oriental evidence to put a son of Aspathines at this sort of level. The fourth admiral is Megabazos son of Megabates. The names are confusing, but Burn[18] has attempted to sort out Herodotus' data. I can contribute what may be another Megabazos (Bakabaduš), satrap in Arachosia and Gandara in 501 to 494, but the attraction of making him a parallel to Gergis is somewhat reduced by the thought that a career in Afghanistan and Baluchistan is not a very satisfactory preparation for being an admiral. I wonder whether the job is not in some sense hereditary. After all, a Megabates is a fairly prominent admiral around 500 (V.32 ff.). Some time late in the reign of Darius he still seems to be described at Persepolis as 'the admiral', Bakabada *MÀ gi-ul-li-ra* (PT 8).[19]

It would be intensely tedious to go down a level, to the commanders of contingents in any detail. I have noted one or two already, and the general impression of reliability remains. To take one name in particular, for his importance in 479 rather than in 480, Artabazos son of Pharnakes, singled out by Burn[20] as a rare commoner, now

---

[17] Cameron (supra note 6) 104.

[18] Burn (supra note 14) 335.

[19] I should note that two late sources (D.S. XI.12.2; Strabo IX.2.9) had Megabates himself as admiral-in-chief in 480.

[20] Burn (supra note 14) 324.

falls nicely into place as son of Pharnakes-Parnaka, Darius' uncle, so prominent at Persepolis and unknown to Greek sources. He would certainly have the social position to argue with Mardonios.

I confess that it is hard to avoid conducting such an investigation without tacit assumptions that Herodotus should be thought right and that the task is to fit other information round him, but, by and large, this does not seem to be an impossible task in this case. I do not see much alternative to the view that there is at least some nucleus, documentary or quasi-documentary, to Herodotus' list, which correlated contingents with real names. There have been many to say that it is impossible that Xerxes should have taken such a motley collection with him, a view strongly combated by Burn.[21] There have been complaints about the difficulties of correlating the national contingents with oriental information, a view most strongly put recently by Armayor.[22] But Armayor has not, at least in print, attacked the commanders' names, and I do not readily see how this could be done.

I do not think that what stands as Xerxes' army-list is a unitary document. It has always been relatively easy to detach the ethnographic notes about the former names of various peoples, particularly those which attempt to tie them into Greek mythology, and most of them have close points of contact with other parts of Herodotus' work,[23] though he does not always tell precisely the same story; Herodotus would be perfectly capable of doing this amount of embroidery for himself. More trouble arises when we consider the weaponry attributed to the national contingents. Here I have considerable sympathy with Armayor, though not all his arguments are equally strong. It is true that Schmidt, in commenting on the Persepolis reliefs,[24] is an extreme case of credulity about Herodotus, tying himself into considerable knots rather than discard Herodotean information. I am satisfied that there is a strong case, as Armayor indicates, for believing that much of this weaponry came from the ethnographic work of Herodotus' predecessor Hecataeus and not from any official list. To restate the point more fully than Armayor has yet done in print, it is at least

[21] Burn (supra note 14) 325-6.

[22] Kimball Armayor, "Herodotus' Catalogues of the Persian Empire," *TAPA* 108 (1978) 1-9.

[23] VII.93 makes an explicit reference to I.171.

[24] E.F. Schmidt, *Persepolis III: The Royal Tombs and Other Monuments* (*OIP* 70, Chicago 1970) 143 ff.

a remarkable coincidence that the two points where we know what Hecataeus said about people's costumes find their exact reflection in Herodotus. Hecataeus (*FGH* 1 F287) said that the Matienoi wore the same costumes as the Paphlagonians; so does Herodotus (VII.72.1). Hecataeus (1 F284) said that the Kissians wore Persian clothing; so does Herodotus (VII.62.2). And there is a further point which I find convincing. At VII.77.1 Herodotus is talking about the Kabelees and says "they had the same equipment as the Cilicians which I shall describe when I get to the Cilicians as I go through." It seems to me that the reasonable inference from this sentence is that Herodotus is taking his information from a written source which had described the Cilicians before the Kabelees, and adapting it to his own purposes which involve a list which has the Cilicans after the Kabelees.

I concede therefore that there is a good deal in the list of Xerxes' army which is not documentary, but this is not the same thing as conceding that there is no documentary core at all. In fact, this may be the single case where it is legitimate to try to unwind Herodotus and disentangle what he gives us into separate strands. It would be gross folly to attempt to extend this in any detail into non-documentary passages where Herodotus has woven his material more closely, but I do not think that we should neglect the general indications provided by this particular case about the way in which he has built up his work and formed first-hand information and the work of his predecessors into a literary narrative.

I come back finally to the documentary core. What kind of list was it and who gave it to Herodotus? I think that there is one more point to be made. There was not simply a list, but someone who transmitted it, embroidering it as he went along with a little extra detail and explanation, about, for example, who was married to whom, who was an Achaemenid, if that was not obvious, and scraps about later careers. We get such extra information for 11 of the 29 contingent commanders. One of these bits (VII.69.2), the longest, is that most amply confirmed by Persepolis, and such extra details are provided for the high command as well. My guess remains that this informant was a Greek. It would however be fair to say that there is a chronological gap before Herodotus can have talked to anybody, and I would not say even now that it was illegitimate to speculate about a written source. I shall not join in.

Fragments of the Preserved Historians — Especially Polybius

WESLEY E. THOMPSON
University of California, Davis

There is a romantic allure to collecting and interpreting fragments of lost works. What could be more pleasurable than reconstructing the plot of *Prometheus Unbound*? And Toni Raubitschek certainly enjoyed himself studying what Theopompus and Theophrastus said about ostracism. But the same interest does not extend to quotations from works which are preserved in their entirety. We know, for instance, who cites Androtion and what sort of information they gain from him, whether it be facts from Athenian history, details of cult, or merely unusual words. But we do not know who quotes Xenophon, nor whether the *Hellenica*, the *Anabasis*, or the *Memorabilia* was the most influential work, nor whether he was cited as the final authority or merely quoted in comparison with Diodorus for fourth century history, Plato for the life of Socrates, and Herodotus for Persian ethnography.[1] Likewise, you can find the fragments of Isaeus without much trouble, but it would be very difficult to find out who saw fit to quote the

---

[1] In the discussion which followed this paper David Lewis remarked that Christopher Tuplin has now done work along these lines, and other participants made useful suggestions. I have tried, however, to reproduce the original form of the lecture.

speeches which have survived and whether they were used as historical sources or literary models. Occasionally it is possible to make some progress along these lines. Hude's *editio maior* contains a full collection of citations from Thucydides, but very little has been done with it.[2]

In the call to the meeting we are asked "what direction research and explanation should take in the coming decades." It seems to me that one useful project for the future would be to collect the "fragments" of Herodotus and Xenophon — and, for that matter, those of the extant orations — and then to exploit this material and the evidence gathered by Hude for Thucydides.

Even now, without the collection process, it is still possible to learn a great deal about one of the major historians — Polybius — by studying the fragments of those books of his which have come down to us complete. Our text of the remaining, fragmentary books is derived almost entirely from two sources, the so-called *Excerpta Antiqua* from the first eighteen books, and the collection of Excerpts taken from the whole work, compiled at the command of the Emperor Constantine Porphyrogenitus. The latter is arranged according to subject matter, such as material to illustrate diplomatic embassies, military stratagems, and plots against kings, subjects which no doubt interested the Emperor Constantine greatly.[3] The rationale for the choice of the *Excerpta Antiqua* has not been adequately determined.

The last half of Polybius' history, as we have it, consists largely of diplomatic history and the internal politics of the Greek cities. One would hardly guess that Polybius was also, perhaps even primarily, a military historian. The reason for this misleading impression is obvious. Most of the text is derived from the Constantinian collection devoted to embassies, and Polybius regularly explains the factional disputes that lead to, or result from, diplomatic missions. Even when there is a war on, our texts of Polybius tell us more about the diplomatic maneuverings than about actual fighting. It's something like preserving Book 5 of Thucydides while throwing away Books 6 and 7. The Third Macedonian War, for example, occupies some fifty-

---

[2] To be sure, David Lewis studied the value of indirect tradition for the text in his 1952 Princeton dissertation, *Towards a Historian's Text of Thucydides*, but I have in mind something different: how later ages used the classical authors.

[3] For a convenient summary of the Constantinian Excerpts cf. Paul Lemerle, *Le premier humanisme byzantin* (Paris 1971) 280-288.

five pages in the Teubner edition. Of these, thirty-three pages are derived from the collection of excerpts *De Legationibus*.[4]

For the same reason we learn very little about *res Asiae* from Polybius. Since the Seleucids were further removed geographically and less dependent politically than mainland Greece, there was much less diplomatic intercourse between them and the Romans, and thus much less material to interest the compiler of the *De Legationibus*. And, of course, he had no concern at all for the fighting which the Seleucids waged. Let us take as our test case this time the Sixth Syrian War, where all but three excerpts are from the *De Legationibus*.[5] Thus we learn how Antiochus Epiphanes justified his declaration of war (28.20), how the Achaeans rejected the call of Lycortas' faction to send troops to the Ptolemies and chose instead to honor the Roman request to mediate a settlement to the conflict (29.23-25), and finally how the Romans ended the war through aggressive diplomacy and their threat to intervene on the side of Egypt (29.27). But we learn nothing at all about how Antiochus came within a whisker of capturing all of Egypt. The closest we come to putting on armor is a fragment preserved by Athenaeus in which Polybius describes Antiochus' victory parade (30.25).

For the purposes of history the selection process of the Constantinian Excerpts is not such a serious matter: we can, after all, obtain a lot of information from Livy and Diodorus about the events which the excerptors omitted. But for the purposes of historiography this method of selection has led to a great distortion, even deformation, of the scope and nature of Polybius' work. It helps to create the impression of a monomaniac, hammering away constantly at the same topic, the Roman manipulation of Greek internal discord, with only an occasional so-called "methodological" digression, in which the author complains mercilessly about the shortcomings of other historians and preaches the need for learning from his own brand of writing history.

In his recent essay, "On Historical Fragments and Epitomes," Brunt says that "even excerpts [as opposed to mere fragments], unless they

---

[4] All references in this paper are to the 1962-1963 reprint of Buettner-Wobst's Teubner edition. The *Bellum Persicum* occupies 27.1-12, 14-16; 28.3-11; and 29.3-21, of which 27.1-8, 14; 28.3-9; and 29.3-4, 10-11, 19 come from the collection of embassies.
[5] 28.18-23; 29.23-27. The other fragments merely tell us that Antiochus was a worthy king (28.18), that it is hard to carry out one's good intentions (29.26), and how Ptolemy VI quit Egypt under the influence of a eunuch (28.21).

are very numerous, substantial, and representative, cannot reveal the *scope* of an author's work. For instance the Constantinian excerpts from Arrian's *Anabasis* come chiefly from the volumes on *Virtue and Vice* and on *Gnomai* and overweight its moralizing and sententious elements."[6] As I have indicated, the main contributor to our version of the second half of Polybius is the *De Legationibus*. The next two major sources are these same collections on *Virtue and Vice*, and on *Gnomai*. The effect of their contribution to the text of Polybius is the same as Brunt describes in the case of Arrian. The difference is that nobody has to depend on these compilations of extracts for his text of Arrian: he can read it straight. But we can have only the kind of Polybius that the Byzantine anthologists chose to preserve.

Brunt adds, "Epitomators in general seem to have aimed not at producing faithful resumés but at recording, sometimes at length, what they thought of most interest, and their principles of selection are at times impenetrable. They do not necessarily offer a faithful miniature of the original as a whole."[7] He cites the summary of Arrian's *Anabasis* made by Bishop Photius. "It occupies," he says, "about a hundred lines of the Teubner text, of which nineteen suffice for the first three books; there is not even a mention of the siege of Tyre. By contrast Photius can list almost all the brides and bridegrooms at the Susa weddings. He distorts the whole economy of the work."[8] Brunt concludes that "'Fragments' and even epitomes reflect the interests of the authors who cite or summarize lost works as much as or more than the characteristics of the works concerned."[9]

Once this is said, it all seems obvious enough, and surely Polybius scholars must be aware of the problem and react accordingly. But I would agree with Brunt that "scholars have often been too precipitate in characterizing and evaluating lost histories on the basis of evidence that is irremediably insufficient, and that in particular too little account is commonly taken of the relevant characteristics of the authors who preserve the 'reliquiae', their reliability in quoting or summarizing, and their own interests and purposes."[10] Even our greatest authority on Polybius, a man who is not only learned but also very perceptive, has not been able to avoid this mistake. At a conference like

[6] *CQ* 74 (1980) 485.
[7] (Supra n. 6) 487.
[8] Ibid.
[9] (Supra n. 6) 494.
[10] (Supra n. 6) 477-478.

this one[11] Professor Walbank was asked "whether we have a clear notion of the criteria according to which the excerpts were made: we cannot assume *a priori* that the tenth century excerptors were interested in the problem of Roman imperialism." Walbank simply replied, "These are important points and the answers are not easy. The interests of the excerptors can, I suppose, be deduced from the actual content of the surviving excerpts." In response, Momigliano suggested a much better way to proceed: to make "a comparison between the excerpts from books i-v and the full text. This, as far as I know, has never been properly done."

This is an excellent idea, to which I return shortly, but first I want to argue that Momigliano has fallen into the same trap which he himself pointed out. In a piece written for *The New York Review of Books* he says that "there are at least two basic facts which [Polybius] underrates. One is the Roman conquest of Spain and the other is the Roman organization of Italy. In either case we may suspect that he was misled by his Greek preoccupations and prejudices."[12] In discussing his first contention he observes, "The decision to remain in Spain and to control it was a compound of economic considerations (mines to explore and lands to colonize) and of instinctive pleasure in power... But if there was inducement to plunder and massacre at pleasure, there was also a danger of demoralization of which the Romans themselves soon became aware. It was to fight corruption in dealing with the Spanish provinces that they first instituted special tribunals for malversation in 149 b.c., and there are other signs that they became uneasy about the behaviour of their generals in the Peninsula. Unless we are misled by the lacunas in Polybius' text, he appears to be insensitive to the problems presented to Rome by its conquest of Spain. There is no sign that he realized that the destruction of Numantia by his friend Scipio raised the same moral problems as the destruction of Corinth and Carthage."

Even if the lay reader actually notices the proviso, "Unless we are misled by the lacunas in Polybius' text...," he will surely ignore it. Clearly Momigliano himself does not believe that in the missing portions of his history Polybius actually did comment on the importance of Spain. He ascribes "Greek preoccupations and prejudices" to

---

[11] Cf. *Entretiens sur l'antiquité classique* XX, *Polybe* (Geneva 1974) 35-36.
[12] See now "The Historian's Skin," in his *Essays in Ancient and Modern Historiography* (Oxford 1977) 75.

Polybius without allowing for the possibility that these are the faults of the epitomators. The military historian M.J.V. Bell also assures the reader that Polybius "was a Greek, not particularly interested in Spain as the balance of his work shows."[13] But is this really the case? In Book 3 Polybius comments on the significance of Spain to the Carthaginians (10.5-6; cf. 35.5-6) and describes some of Hannibal's fighting there (13.5-14.10 and 17). And in his second preface he announces that, following his exposition of the Roman constitution, he will show how it made possible the reconquest of Italy and Sicily and the subjugation of the Spaniards and Celts (3.2.6). He also promises "an account of the subsequent policy of the conquerors and their method of universal rule, as well as of the various opinions and appreciations of their rulers entertained by the subjects, and finally I must describe what were the prevailing and dominant tendencies and ambitions of the various peoples in their private and public life."[14] Surely this proves that Polybius had an interest in Spain which the excerptors did not share. He goes on to say (3.5.1) that he will describe the Roman war against the Celtiberians and Vaccaei, but once again the compiler of the *De Legationibus* has omitted this conflict since his task was to record negotiating, not fighting.

To summarize, then, when Oswyn Murray says, "Certainly Polybius is the greatest surviving political historian of the period, and our accounts [of Hellenistic historiography] will always to some extent be biased towards his preoccupations,"[15] I would quarrel with the word "his." Certainly you cannot excerpt what the author himself did not include, and surely Greece was more important than Spain to Polybius, but the almost total purgation of Spain from the text of Polybius shows that our accounts of Hellenistic history writing are biased toward the prejudices and preoccupations of the men who chopped and whittled Polybius down to manageable size.

When we ask "what direction research and explanation should take in the coming decades," I would answer that we should put first things first. Before anyone undertakes an analysis of Polybius similar to the

---

[13] "Tactical Reform in the Roman Republican Army," *Historia* 14 (1965) 414.

[14] 3.4.6; all translations of Polybius in this paper are taken from the Loeb edition of W. R. Paton. Of course, Polybius covered the fighting in Spain during the Second Punic War, but the excerptors managed to ignore such an important event as the death of the two Scipios.

[15] "Herodotus and Hellenistic Culture," *CQ* 66 (1972) 212.

studies of Herodotus and Thucydides which have appeared lately, we need to determine the nature of the bias that underlies our text of Polybius, along the lines suggested by Momigliano. It is necessary to study what the compiler of the *Excerpta Antiqua*, for instance, chose from the first five books and more importantly — what he omitted from his collection. This should provide a clear indication of what he has omitted from Books 6-18. One must then compare what he did retain from those books to see whether his standards change in the course of his work. One would do the same for the various volumes of the Constantinian Excerpts to discover on what basis items were chosen for the *De Legationibus, On Virtue and Vice, Gnomai*, and the rest.[16]

This would be a vast undertaking, for the Constantinian Excerpts contain huge chunks of other historians besides Polybius, running to over 1500 pages. Ideally, to understand the mentality of the excerptors one should know his Herodotus so well that in reading through the Constantinian Excerpts of that author he will know what is missing and comprehend the full extent of the loss. And he will know his Thucydides too, and also his Xenophon. The task requires a tremendous power of imagination, for it is one thing to analyze the texts we have before us, but something altogether different to appreciate the significance of what has been lost.

As an example of the sort of research I have in mind, the remainder of my paper will be given over to an analysis of the way the *Excerpta Antiqua* were chosen. Since we are concerned today with the direction of future research, it seems more appropriate to present an ongoing project rather than a completed one. Even better, this is not a topic where the answer was known in advance and merely needed to be documented: at the beginning of this line of inquiry I had not the slightest idea of what I would find.

First it would be standard procedure to outline current ideas on the subject, but in this case I have only found one scholar who even addresses the question of how the *Excerpta Antiqua* were compiled. John Moore, who has studied the manuscript tradition of Polybius, asked himself why the *Excerpta Antiqua* are drawn only from the first eighteen books. "No satisfactory hypothesis has so far been advanced as

---

[16] Kenneth Sacks, *Polybius on the Writing of History* (Berkeley and Los Angeles 1981) 11-20, has made a start by determining what percentage of "methodological" passages from Books 1-5 appear in the collection of *Gnomai*.

to why they should have ended at this point, but consideration of content suggests the following as a possibility. By the end of XVIII the excerpts had not merely covered the history to the end of the Second Punic War, but had also dealt with the conflict with Philip V which was an almost inevitable result of relations between Rome and Philip during the Second Punic War, and had brought the narrative down to a suitable climax with the battle of Cynoscephalae and the Isthmus declaration of 196 B.C. The presence of some material dealing with other areas would be natural, granted Polybius' method of writing history."[17] That is, he assumes that the *Excerpta Antiqua* constitute, in Brunt's words, "a faithful miniature" of the first half of the *Histories*. The inadequacy of such an explanation will be apparent as soon as one realizes that it is the *De Legationibus*, not the *Excerpta Antiqua*, which preserves the *senatus consultum* on the freedom of the Greeks and the joyous celebration of it at the Isthmian Games.[18]

To give some idea of the type of material which the selector of the Excerpts omits I have surveyed Book 3, where the events are well known.[19] He does not include Polybius' introduction (1), which is pretty much a repetition of what he has already copied from the beginning of Book 1 (1.1-3.5), nor does he transcribe the list of wars and other topics which Polybius proposes to treat (2-5). He ignores the theoretical discussion of what constitutes the causes of wars as distinct from the pretexts (6-7), and Polybius' specific application of his doctrine to the Second Punic War (8-15). Thus—a point of some significance for Momigliano's case—the excerptor does not notice the growth of Carthaginian power in Spain (13-15.1), which Polybius regards as one of the causes of the war (10.6). The compiler then skips over the *dikaiologia*, in which Polybius presents the arguments about where guilt for the war lies (20-21) and offers his own interpretation of the three treaties between Rome and Carthage (22-30). The selector also omits Polybius' argument for the value of studying cause and effect (31) and his *apologia* for the enormous length of his work (32).

When the historian finally reaches the military portion of Book 3, the compiler ignores Hannibal's preparations, including campaigns to secure Carthage's hold on Spain (33.5-35). Nor does he copy

---

[17] "Polybiana," *GRBS* 12 (1971) 428.

[18] 18.46; cf. Buettner-Wobst's apparatus.

[19] The most convenient list of the *Excerpta Antiqua* from 1-5 is found in Buettner-Wobst's edition, II, pp. LXIII-LXIV.

Polybius' account of Hannibal's troop strength (35.7-8; 56.4), which — the historian proudly informs the reader (33.17-18) — is based on an inscription set up by Hannibal himself. Likewise he ignores the distances of Hannibal's route, much of which Polybius painstakingly calculated and retraced in person (39; 48.12). He skips over most of the crossing of the Rhone (42-46) and the Alps (50-56).

Once Hannibal reaches Italy, the compiler ignores the basic strategy of the war, including Hannibal's decision to move away from friendly territory and fight the war on hostile ground (78.5), his instigation of revolt throughout Italy,[20] and — in particular — the motive and significance of his attack on the plain of Capua (90.10-12). The excerptor also overlooks the counter-strategy devised by Fabius Maximus (89.2-90.5) and Roman attempts to take the offensive outside Italy (76; 96-99). We search in vain for Polybius' judgment that the cause of Rome's ultimate victory was its *politeia* (118.7-9).

We also miss some of the particulars of the action, including the first battle in Italy (65), the Roman retreat to the Trebia (66-68), and Hannibal's various marches through the peninsula,[21] especially the grueling three and one-half day passage of the swamp lying before Trasimene (79).

As you can see, the excerptor has badly defaced Polybius' narrative, and we can expect that the result will be the same in those books where the *Excerpta Antiqua* constitute the main source for our texts.

What, then, has he included? Only matters military and geographical. He transcribes Polybius' discussion of the three continents and their boundaries (36.6-38.5), as well as his geography of the Rhone and the Alps (47.2-4). His military excerpts include the great battles of the Trebia (70.1-75.4), Trasimene (80.1-85.4), and Cannae (108.2-117.6), which might indicate that his work was directed to the general reader who wanted to know the most significant events of the war, without the burden of superfluous detail and the vast quantity of turgid prose Polybius serves up. But in reading the excerpts from Book 3, I developed the suspicion that our man was really more interested in military stratagems than famous battles, and that suspicion was confirmed in studying the other books.

In the very first excerpt from Book 3, Polybius describes the Roman attack on the island of Pharos, in which they first put men ashore

---

[20] Cf. 67; 69.1-4; 77.3-7; 118.1-5.
[21] 86.8-11; 88.3-6; 90.7-10.

at an uninhabited spot and then sail brazenly into the main harbor. When the defenders sally out to meet the ships, the commandoes ambush them.[22] Or take the crossings of the Rhone and the Alps. The excerptor omits all the fighting at the Rhone (42-43) and simply copies out Hannibal's device for transporting the elephants by tying rafts together (45.6-46.7). He does not even include the actual crossing of the panic stricken animals (46.8-12); he is solely interested in the *mechane*. It took Hannibal fifteen days to cross the Alps, but the compiler has preserved the activity of a single day (50.1-51.11). Hannibal sends troops ahead during the night to seize the peaks above a certain pass. This first discourages the natives from attacking, but when they see the baggage train in difficulty, they make their assault. Hannibal is then able to attack them in turn from the high ground. Other obvious stratagems by the Carthaginian are his staging of a gladiatorial contest between two prisoners of war to demonstrate to his own men that it is better to die fighting than to submit to slavery, and his trick of attaching torches to the horns of cattle so that Fabius Maximus follows the animals while Hannibal's troops escape in the opposite direction.[23]

Hannibal wins many of his victories by ambush, and the excerptor includes two such stratagems based on the principle of knowing the personality of the opposing general. Chapter 81, included in the *Excerpta*, contains Polybius' reflections on the subject in general: "For there is no denying that he who thinks that there is anything more essential to a general than the knowledge of his opponent's principles and character, is both ignorant and foolish." One must see "what are the weak spots that can be discovered in [the opponent's] mind," and exploit such faults as sloth, drinking, lust, cowardice, and stupidity. "Rashness... and undue boldness and blind anger, as well as vaingloriousness and conceit, are easy to be taken advantage of by his enemy and are most dangerous to his friends; for such a general is the easy victim of all manner of plots, ambushes, and cheatery. Therefore the leader who will soonest gain a decisive victory, is he who is able to perceive the faults of others and to choose that manner and means of attacking the enemy which will take full advantage of the weaknesses of their commander."

[22] 18.10-19.8; 19.12-13. At 18.9 Polybius calls this attack a *strategema*. This is one of the few excerpts where part of Polybius' text is omitted, viz., 19.9-10, which tells of the later career of Demetrius of Pharos.

[23] 62.2-63.14; 92.1-94.7.

Hannibal puts these precepts into practice by learning the character of Flaminius and Marcus Minucius. In a passage from the *Excerpta* which calls to mind Thucydides' description of Cleon at Amphipolis, Polybius says that Hannibal found out that "Flaminius was a thorough mob-courtier and demagogue, with no talent for the practical conduct of war and exceedingly self-confident withal. [Thus] he calculated that if he passed by the Roman army and advanced into the country in his front, the Consul would on the one hand never look on while he laid it waste for fear of being jeered at by his soldiery; and on the other hand he would be so grieved that he would be ready to follow anywhere, in his anxiety to gain the coming victory himself without waiting for the arrival of his colleague."[24] Flaminius then follows Hannibal into the trap at Trasimene, a passage which the selector transcribed in full. He also chose to include a relatively minor affair in which "Hannibal... was aware of the rivalry [between the two dictators Fabius and Minucius] and of Marcus' impulsiveness and ambition."[25] Now Minucius was also puffed up by a minor victory, so Hannibal devised a plan to take advantage of his over-confidence. He placed men in ambush during the night and the next day began to fortify a hill that lay between his position and the Roman camp, "well knowing that owing to his previous achievement Minucius would instantly advance to frustrate this project." When the Romans came out to dispute possession of the hill, Hannibal unleashed his men from the hiding-place.

Even though some of the excerpts from Book 3 are quite colorful and might interest the general reader, the evidence is strong that the excerptor was preparing a book with a fairly narrow focus for those concerned with military tactics rather than simply a condensed version of an overly long historical classic. In university terms, he was compiling a text for a course in military science, not ancient history.

In the other books where our text is complete, the epitomator is more catholic in his taste.[26] Once again we find the geographical passages: descriptions of Italy (2.14.4-17.8),[27] Byzantium and the Black Sea (4.38.1-45.8), and Media (5.44.3-11). In addition, we find selections that seem to correspond in type to the material which appears in the Constantinian Excerpts. We have character sketches of

---

[24] 80.3-4; cf. Thuc. 5.7.1-2.
[25] 104.1-105.10. This illustrates the same point as the *gnome* copied at 1.84.6-10.
[26] See supra n. 19.
[27] He omits the anthropology and history of the Gauls (17.9-22.6).

Aratus (4.8.1-12) and Philip V (4.24.4-7; 5.9.1-12.8), the sort of thing that appears in the collection *On Virtue and Vice*,[28] and about a dozen general observations that could be classified as *gnomai*, such as, "So great is the difference both to individuals and to states between carefulness and wisdom on the one hand, and folly with negligence on the other, that in the latter case good fortune actually inflicts damage, while in the former disaster is the cause of profit."[29]

We have the military excerpts, of course, including two set pieces, Sellasia (2.65.6-69.11) and Raphia,[30] and a trio of lesser encounters, which — at first sight — seem to illustrate different types of fighting that a general must master. One is the battle of Caphyae (4.11.1-13.2), where Polybius stresses the importance of terrain, criticizing Aratus for his failure to use his heavy infantry against the Aetolian light infantry in the plain, where he would have had the advantage. In another excerpt (2.25.1-31.7) the Gauls are caught between two Roman armies and accordingly line up with one half of their army facing one way, and the other half facing the opposite direction. Finally, a battle between Philip V and the Spartans (5.22.1-23.6) seems to be about breaking through a strong defensive position.

The selector has also chosen two stratagems devised by Hamilcar Barca (1.75.5-76.9). Noticing that the Bagradas River, which blocked his advance, became very shallow at its mouth when the wind blew strongly upon it at certain times, Hamilcar was able to lead his army across at just the right spot and just the right moment. Thereupon he defeated his opponents, who attacked from two sides, by feigning

[28] The Aratus excerpt and the second passage about Philip are, in fact, part of that collection. Perhaps the section on music in Arcadian education (4.20.1-21.4) was chosen to illustrate the character of the Arcadian people, for part of it also appears in *Virtue and Vice*.

[29] 5.88.3; cf. also 1.81.5-11; 1.83.2-4; 1.84.6-10; 2.7.1-3; 4.27.1-8; 4.31.3-8; 4.60.8-10; 4.74.3-7; 4.77.2-4; 4.85.3-6; 4.87.3-4; 5.26.12-13; 5.32.1-33.8; 5.75.2-6; 5.90.5-8; and 5.104.1-11 (which I take to illustrate the view that people must close ranks against the foreigner). Notice especially 5.75.2-6, "...And indeed it seems to me that man, who is supposed to be the most cunning of all animals, is in fact the most easily duped. For how many camps and fortresses, how many great cities have not been betrayed by this means?... The reason of this is that we have not ready to hand in our memories the various disasters that have overtaken others... although we can gain from this experience from study of history and inquiry..."

[30] 5.64.1-65.11 and 79.3-86.7; this is the one displacement in the text. The epitomator wanted to keep the *sententia* which appears at 5.75.2-6 but did not want to interrupt the battle narrative. He, therefore, placed the *gnome* after 86.7.

retreat and—once the enemy broke ranks to pursue—by wheeling around into battle formation.

There are three passages of general historical interest: the preface to Book 1 (1.1-3.5), Polybius' summary of the growth of Roman power up to the First Punic War (1.6.1-7.11), and a *gnome* emphasizing the importance and difficulty of writing a universal history (5.32.1-33.8). Finally, we have a seemingly inexplicable choice about the arrival of a Numidian defector to the camp of Hamilcar (1.77.6-78.15).

Despite exceptions, it is clear that we have a military, not a political, compendium. The compiler has no interest in the history of the Achaean League, the tyrants of Sparta, or the social question in Greece. Even the military selections are not representative, as they favor tactics over strategy. The selector entirely omits the First Punic War in favor of the attack on Pharos, includes nothing to explain the Mercenary War of which the battle of the Bagradas is part, and has no interest in long marches, such as Hannibal's great treks or the lightning campaigns of Philip V through the Peloponnese which drew the admiration of Polybius.[31] His prime concern is what Polybius calls "plots, ambushes, and cheatery," and this interest grows more pronounced in the remaining books.

Instead of going through the whole of the *Excerpta Antiqua*, I have chosen to compare the selections from Books 7-11 with those from the first pentad. We find once again extracts about geography[32] and observations on the character of such men as Aratus (8.12), Antiochus the Great (11.34), and Hasdrubal (11.1.2-3.6).[33] The excerptor is especially interested in the character of Scipio Africanus, how he relies on planning and does not trust to luck (10.2-17), and how he wins the support of his troops by his own moderation in the treatment of

---

[31] Cf. 4.67.6-80.16; 5.17.8-19.8.

[32] 7.6 (Leontini); 9.27 (Agrigentum); 9.43 (the Euphrates); 10.1 (Tarentum); 10.27 (Ecbatana); 10.48 (the Oxus and Tanais). The *Excerpta Antiqua* from Books 7-11 are listed by John M. Moore, *The Manuscript Tradition of Polybius* (Cambridge 1965) 55-56; cf. also Buettner-Wobst's apparatus. In this paper I ignore the short selections (almost always *sententiae*) copied in the margin of the main manuscript. In Books 7-11 the selector usually copies a lengthy passage in its entirety, including material which is not germane to his main topic. Thus it is not always clear why he has made the selection, and in some cases he may have been attracted by a combination of features, such as episode which involves a clever stratagem and also throws light on a general's personality.

[33] Cf. also 10.41-42 (Philip V); 11.9-10 (Philopoemen); 11.19 (Hannibal).

women prisoners (10.18-19) and his refusal of kingship (10.40).[34] There is one major battle, Philopoemen's victory at Mantinea (11.11-18), one document, Hannibal's treaty with Philip (7.9), and at least one embassy speech (11.4-6).[35] We also find a number of *gnomai*,[36] including two historiographical passages. In one Polybius again emphasizes the need for universal history (8.1-2); in the other (9.1-2) he justifies his omission of the entertaining in favor of the useful, which is, of course, the excerptor's own creed.

By far the most prominent feature of the second pentad is the large number of stratagems. Their importance to the excerptor is best demonstrated by his inclusion of stratagems which are almost identical to those which he copied from Books 1-5. A campaign of Antiochus[37] corresponds to that portion of Hannibal's crossing of the Alps which the selector included in his book. Hannibal learned that the natives guarded the passes by day and returned home at night, and thus was able to seize the peaks in their absence. Antiochus twice found barbarians guarding passes and by occupying the peaks was able to drive them out with a shower of missiles (10.29.3-31.3). Later in his journey, hearing that some other natives guarded a river crossing during the day but went home at night, he rode ahead and seized the spot when they had retired for the evening. Then he bravely fought off their counter-attacks (10.49). Antiochus' Anabasis lasted some six years, but apart from the capture of a fortified town (10.31.6-13) these exploits of the king are the only actions that caught the selector's eye.

Again in the first pentad the Romans at Pharos, and Hannibal in his duel with Marcus Minucius, first set an ambush and then lured the enemy out of a protected position by provocatively dispatching troops in plain sight. So the *Excerpta Antiqua* from Book 8 contain a story of how Philip V caused his own men to suffer a defeat in the open field so that the garrison left the Acrolissus in quest of booty, only to fall into his ambush.[38] And the excerptor chose to preserve

---

[34] 10.34-38.6 is mostly about his negotiations with the Spaniards.

[35] It is not entirely clear to me whether the excerptor included 9.28-39 as a pair of opposing embassy speeches or as indicators of the character of the rulers of Macedon and the people of Aetolia; cf. supra n. 28.

[36] 7.12; 9.10; 9.40.2-3; 10.25.

[37] 10.27-31, 48-49; 11.34. On this expedition see Édouard Will, *Histoire politique du monde hellénistique*, II (Nancy 1967) 42-59.

[38] 13-14; at 13.4 Polybius calls Philip's action a stratagem.

a battle in which Scipio lured the Spaniards into a meadow by plac-
ing cattle there as bait.[39] Just as Hamilcar noticed that the winds made
the Bagradas shallow at a certain spot, so Scipio observed that low
tide exposed a land bridge to a place from which the citadel of New
Carthage could be climbed. He told his men that Neptune promised
him in a dream to help the Romans, and the dream seemed to come
true when (just on schedule) the waters receded, opening the fortress
to attack (10.8.6-7; 11.7, 14).

After taking the trouble to record Hannibal's device of joining rafts
together to ferry elephants, the excerptor now copies Polybius' account of how the Romans tied ships together at the siege of Syracuse
in order to support giant war machines. He also preserved Polybius'
detailed description of these implements as well as the ingenious devices
which Archimedes prepared for the defense.[40] He also included the
description of Philip's war machine at Echinus, a kind of moving
scaffolding with troops stationed on three floors (9.41).

And there are new stratagems. Polybius himself uses the word
(11.22.1) in connection with Scipio's two tricks that won the battle
of Ilipa (11.20-24): first he brought his army out to fight before the
Carthaginians had a chance to eat and then stationed his best men
on the wings with the unreliable Spaniards in the middle. The excerptor also transcribed the battle of Baecula, in which Scipio again
attacked on the wings while holding his center in reserve (10.39).

In another selection Polybius recounts Hannibal's march on Rome
aimed at drawing off the Roman army besieging Capua, and com-
pares it with Epaminondas' march on Sparta, which forced the
defenders of Mantinea to leave it unguarded (9.3-9).

One of the collections of Constantinian Excerpts consisted of
stratagems. Although it has not survived, we do know that one of
the items was a passage in which Polybius describes how Philopoemen

---

[39] 11.31-33. In this battle the Roman cavalry took the enemy in the rear and bottled
them up in a narrow valley, just as Hannibal did at Trasimene. Following 33.6 the
excerptor omitted the rest of Scipio's Spanish campaign (cf. Livy 28.34-37) and tacked
on 33.7-8 as an epilogue, showing how Scipio's brilliant achievements resulted in
a triumph. He did exactly the same thing at 3.18.10-19.8, adding 19.12-13 to show
how the conqueror of Pharos celebrated a triumph.

[40] 8.4-7. The excerptor did not include ch. 3, which explains the historical circumstances of the siege.

trained his men in all the various cavalry maneuvers.[41] This selection also appears in the *Excerpta Antiqua* (10.23), as does a passage in which Scipio trains his forces at New Carthage (10.20).

Hannibal's assault on Tarentum (8.24.4-34.13) involves a series of stratagems: the way the traitors arrange to come and go at will by pretending to hunt or pillage (24.9-13; 25.4-11); Hannibal's secret march on the city from a distance of three days, which he capped off by arresting everyone outside the town to prevent detection (26); and his device of hauling ships overland from the harbor to the outer sea in order to blockade the Roman garrison (34).

Finally, the capture of Sardes, based — like many of these stratagems — on the principle of hitting the enemy when and where he least expects it. Buried in Polybius' account of the battle of the Trebia is an observation (3.71.2-3) that teaches this lesson: "the Romans, while very suspicious of thickly-wooded ground, which the Celts usually chose for their ambuscades, were not at all afraid of flat and treeless places, not being aware that they are better adapted than woods for the concealment and security of an ambush." Three times, then, in the second pentad the excerptor found material to illustrate that a citadel can be taken at its strongest point, where no one would expect an attack. Philip took the Acrolissus because, relying on its natural strength, the enemy set only a few men to guard it (8.13.9) and the king was able to fool them. At New Carthage Scipio attacked at a spot which was usually under water and so left unguarded (10.14.13-14). And Sardes was taken when one of Antiochus' men saw that vultures and other birds alighted on a portion of the wall of the citadel. He inferred that the defenders were not standing guard there, relying instead on the sheerness of the rock wall. That, of course, is where the attackers scaled the heights and entered the city (7.15-18).

The key to the selection process of the *Excerpta Antiqua* comes, I think, in a passage from Book 9: "The accidents attendant on military projects require much circumspection, but success is in every case possible if the steps we take to carry out our plans are soundly reasoned out. That in military operations what is achieved openly and by force is much less than what is done by stratagem and the use of opportunity, can easily be learnt from the history of former wars" (12.1-2). So victory in war is won by the general who — like Scipio — relies on

---

[41] At the end of 10.22 the scribe of *Virtue and Vice* instructs the reader to seek in the collection of stratagems for the continuation of the text, i.e., what is now ch. 23.

planning and does not trust to luck and knows how to employ stratagems. But the successful leader must master other elements of war, for the quotation continues (12.3-5), "And it is no less easy to be convinced by facts that in those actions depending on the choice of opportunity failure is far more frequent than success. Nor can anyone doubt that most of the failures are due either to error or to negligence on the part of the commander. We must therefore inquire in what such faults consist."

He then proceeds to show the practical importance of astronomy and geometry to a commander,[42] noting, for instance, that Philip V and Cleomenes missed a rendezvous with men who planned to betray their own cities, because each king neglected to figure the time of nightfall according to the season (9.18). Throughout his collection from 7-11 the excerptor has made sure to include other admonitions to would-be leaders. One of the *gnomai* which he copied from Book 1 says, in effect, that being a soldier is one thing, but being a general is another.[43] Thus he also records Polybius' advice not to become involved in minor skirmishes, such as led to the death of the consul Marcellus (10.32-33.7), but to manage the broader concerns of a campaign, as exemplified in the excerpt on how Philopoemen rode sometimes bravely at the head of the cavalry, but then wisely dropped to the rear or inspected the center of the corps in order to gain a view of the whole situation (10.24). When Scipio fights at New Carthage he has three shieldbearers to ward off missiles (10.13.1-5). The Excerpts also include Polybius' teaching that a general should not rashly entrust himself to his enemies, illustrated by the fates of Ti. Sempronius Gracchus and Achaeus.[44] And while some might prefer to view the episode as an indicator of Scipio's character, I would cite as an example of how to avoid danger the excerpt (11.25-30) in which he puts down a mutiny among his troops through a combination of rhetoric and ruthlessness.

[42] 12-20. In the margin of the main manuscript an annotator titles this section, "That it is fitting for a general to practice astronomy and geometry." In ch. 20 Polybius notes the usefulness of geometry for laying out camps, and the excerptor copied the discussion of the Roman camp at 6.27-32. He also preserved 9.26a, about the use of geometry to estimate the size of a camp or city.

[43] 1.84.6-10; he copied the same notion at 3.105.9 in recording a Hannibalic stratagem.

[44] 8.15-21, 35-36; at 21.10 Achaeus is cited as a "useful example to those who came after," since despite all his precautions he was still taken.

The excerptor includes a long discussion of the Roman method of dividing booty, which Polybius recommends as a safety measure (10.16-17.5). Since under the Greek method, "most of the men start pillaging, commanders cannot maintain any control and run the risk of disaster, and indeed many who have been successful in their object have, after capturing the enemy's camp or a town, not only been driven out but have met with complete disaster simply for the above reason." The selector clearly shares the historian's didactic purposes, for the passage ends, "Commanders should therefore exercise the utmost care and foresight about this matter, so that as far as is possible the hope of equal participation in the booty... may be common to all."

One final selection shows clearly that we are dealing with a military handbook and not a faithful miniature, viz., Polybius' comparison of his own system of fire signals with the one recommended by Aeneas Tacticus (10.43-47). The excerptor allotted almost as much space to this item as to the famous description of the Roman constitution in Book 6 (11.11-18.8).

Is it credible, then, that during the tenth century someone would compile a series of excerpts from Polybius to serve as a textbook of tactics? The answer is clearly, yes, for the great textual critic A. Dain has observed that the common Byzantine practice of reworking classical literature (*retractatio*) was a response "to the need to adapt an ancient work to new conditions."[45] The Emperor Constantine himself writes that he regularly took certain books with him on campaign: books on generalship, weaponry, and history, especially Polyaenus and Syrianus.[46] Five abridgments of Polyaenus were available during this period, and his stratagems were rearranged according to type to make them more useful.[47] The *Excerpta Antiqua* are the result of reworking Polybius in the same way.

The topics chosen from Polybius are not merely useful, they are the main concerns of Byzantine commanders. According to Toynbee's excellent analysis of military handbooks of the tenth century, the primary Byzantine tactic was to follow marauding invaders and cut them off at the pass, seizing the heights with light-armed troops who

---

[45] "Les cinq adaptations byzantines des 'Stratagèmes' de Polyen," *REA* 33 (1931) 321.

[46] *De Caerimoniis* 1.Appendix.467 Reiske (reprinted in Migne, *PG* CXII).

[47] Dain (supra n. 45) 321-345. On the practical application of Polybius in the West see Momigliano (supra. n. 12) 91-93.

would rain missiles (especially arrows) down on the enemy.[48] This is why the only excerpt from the crossing of the Alps is Hannibal's occupation of the heights, and why the selector recorded Antiochus' seizure of mountain peaks and a river crossing. When the Byzantines raided Muslim lands, says Toynbee,[49] "The most difficult and dangerous of all contingencies for an East Roman Army is to find that a kleisoúra on the Army's line of retreat from enemy territory has been occupied by the enemy. Keep away from any occupied kleisoúra. It is the terrain, not the enemy himself, that creates the danger. Terrain can enable a weaker force to defeat a stronger. If you can, compel the enemy to evacuate the kleisoúra by sending infantry through other kleisoúrai, that he has not occupied, to take him in the rear. If the enemy cannot be forced or tempted to evacuate, and if his position is impregnable, take one of the side-roads." This would explain the excerptor's interest in Hannibal's escape from the plain of Capua with his trick of attaching torches to the horns of cattle. It would also explain why he included a description of Philip V's victory over the Spartans (5.22.1-23.6). The King was returning north after ravaging Laconia (5.19) and found his way blocked since Sparta lay on his left and the Eurotas and some hills on his right. The forces within the city could attack his flank as he marched past, and Lycurgus had occupied the hills. Since there were no side roads, Philip had to force the position, driving his opponents from the heights.

I originally thought that the selector included the battle in which the Romans attack the Gauls from the front and the rear (2.25.1-31.7) as an example of how to manage fighting on two fronts, but now we can see the real reason for this excerpt: the Gauls were heading home with an enormous haul of booty when a second Roman army unexpectedly arrived by sea at Pisa and then seized the pass through which the Gauls had to proceed.

Sir Charles Oman says, "Of the spirit of chivalry there was not a spark in the Byzantine... [He] was equally remote from the haughty contempt for sleights and tricks which had inspired the ancient

---

[48]   Arnold Toynbee, *Constantine Porphyrogenitus and his World* (London 1973) 109-111, 283, 306, 314-315. Since there is some question whether the handbooks reveal genuine contemporary practice (Toynbee, 294-297), I have added some actual examples from Byzantine history which show the implementation of their teachings.

[49]   (Supra n. 48) 306.

Romans, and from the chivalrous ideals which grew to be at once
the strength and the weakness of the Teutonic West... They considered
it absurd to expend stores, money, and the valuable lives of veteran
soldiers in achieving by force an end that could equally well be obtained by skill."[50] It is in this tradition that our excerptor copied down
Polybius' observation (9.12.2) that "in military operations what is
achieved openly and by force is much less than what is done by
stratagem and the use of opportunity." The Byzantine, according to
Sir Charles, "had a strong predilection for stratagems, ambushes, and
simulated retreats." We have already seen the selector's great interest
in ambushes and in Hamilcar's feigned retreat at the Bagradas. A
favorite device of the Byzantine handbooks, and one actually used
against the pretender John Bryennius, is to send out a small force
to attack the enemy or to ravage his territory.[51] When they encounter
resistance, they flee pell-mell, and lead their pursuers into an ambush. The *Excerpta Antiqua* include two battles (3.104-105; 8.13-14)
in which commanders use their men as bait.

One of the main themes of the handbooks is the need to exercise
troops in military maneuvers and discipline well before heading off
to meet the foe, and Leo the Deacon on at least half a dozen occasions mentions that a general prepared his forces this way.[52] This interest accounts for the preservation of 10.23, where Philopoemen exercises his men. The Byzantine use of fire signals explains the selection of Polybius' discussion of this device.[53] Another passage which
only begins to reveal its meaning in the light of Byzantine *tactica* is
Polybius' account of Hamilcar's conduct in the Mercenary War
(1.77.6-78.15), beginning with the arrival at his camp of an African
noble seeking to defect. As Toynbee puts it, "The interrogation of
prisoners and deserters is also considered to be indispensable,"[54] and
Polybius shows Hamilcar examining the young man who wants to

---

[50] *A History of the Art of War in the Middle Ages*, I (New York 1924) 201. The next
quotation comes from the following page.
[51] *De velitatione bellica* 138; 140; 149; 153 Hase (reprinted in Migne, *PG* CXVII);
Nicephorus Bryennius, *Histories* 4.10-12. One of the tricks recommended resembles
the device Philip used at Lissus; cf. R. Vari (ed.), *Incerti Scriptoris Byzantini Saeculi
X. Liber de Re Militari* (Leipzig 1901) ch. 26.
[52] Toynbee (supra n. 48) 316-317; Leo Diaconus, *History* 1.9; 2.1; 3.1; 3.9; 4.1;
6.11; 6.13; 7.3; 7.9; 10.9.
[53] Toynbee (supra n. 48) 299.
[54] Ibid.

become his helper, as well as Antiochus scrutinizing the Cretan who offers to betray Achaeus (8.17.2). Finally, we notice the similarity between Hannibal's march on Rome, intended to relieve Capua, and "a brilliantly successful diversionary raid into Cilicia that was made by Nikêphóros Phokás the elder" which forced "the Cilician Moslems to raise their siege of the East Roman fortress Místheia."[55]

It is easy to believe that the *Excerpta Antiqua* were chosen for their similarity to Byzantine military practices. That in itself does not mean that a Byzantine commander was consciously following Polybius whenever he outfoxed the enemy, but it does mean that the study of Polybius, Polyaenus, and handbooks which go back to the Roman Empire[56] helped shape the overall outlook of a tenth century general.

There are a few topics remaining to complete this research project. We need to examine the character sketches in the *Excerpta Antiqua* more closely to see whether they correspond to those portions of Byzantine manuals which discuss the qualities of a good general. Professor Pearson, I am sure, will want to know what attracted the compiler to preserve part of the historiographical Book 12. Perhaps the largest problem of all is Book 6. I always used to wonder why anyone would be interested in that tedious description of the Roman camp. Now I know: Byzantine handbooks are filled with similar descriptions which go back — by the process of *retractatio* — to Polybius.[57] Now, paradoxically, I wonder why the man who showed so little interest in politics chose to preserve Polybius' discussion of constitutional cycles and his description of the Roman *politeia*.

---

[55] Toynbee (supra n. 48) 317.

[56] Toynbee (supra n. 48) 292-293; for Byzantine reworking of an even earlier military writer see J.-R. Vieillefond, "Adaptations et paraphrases du *Commentaire* d'Énée le Tacticien," *RevPhil*[3] 6 (1932) 24-36.

[57] Toynbee (supra n. 48) 306-310.